CliffsNotes™

Dubliners

By Adam Sexton, M.F.A.

IN THIS BOOK

- Learn about the Life and Background of the Author
- Read about all the stories in *Dubliners*
- Examine in-depth "Araby"
- Examine in-depth "The Dead"
- Enhance your understanding with the Critical Essay
- Reinforce what you learn with CliffsNotes Review
- Find additional information to further your study in CliffsNotes Resource Center and online at www.cliffsnotes.com

OIL C~
2 CENTRAL AVENUE
OIL CITY, PA. 16301

WILEY
Wiley Publishing, Inc.

About the Author

Adam Sexton is a teacher and freelance writer. He received a B.A. in English from the University of Pennsylvania and an M.F.A. in Writing from Columbia University. He lives in Brooklyn, NY.

Publisher's Acknowledgments

Editorial

Project Editor: Ben Nussbaum
Acquisitions Editor: Greg Tubach
Copy Editor: Katie Robinson
Glossary Editors: The editors and staff at Webster's New World Dictionaries

Composition

Indexer: TECHBOOKS Production Services
Proofreader: TECHBOOKS Production Services
Wiley Publishing, Inc. Composition Services

CliffsNotes™ *Dubliners*

Published by:
Wiley Publishing, Inc.
909 Third Avenue
New York, NY 10022
www.wiley.com

Note: If you purchased this book without a cover, you should be aware that this book is stolen property. It was reported as "unsold and destroyed" to the publisher, and neither the author nor the publisher has received any payment for this "stripped book."

Copyright © 2003 Wiley Publishing, Inc. New York, New York

Library of Congress Cataloging in Publication Data available from Publisher

ISBN: 0-7645-3715-6

Printed in the United States of America

10 9 8 7 6 5 4 3 2 1

1O/RU/QU/QT/IN

Published by Wiley Publishing, Inc., New York, NY
Published simultaneously in Canada

No part of this publication may be reproduced, stored in a retrieval system, or transmitted in any form or by any means, electronic, mechanical, photocopying, recording, scanning, or otherwise, except as permitted under Sections 107 or 108 of the 1976 United States Copyright Act, without either the prior written permission of the Publisher, or authorization through payment of the appropriate per-copy fee to the Copyright Clearance Center, 222 Rosewood Drive, Danvers, MA 01923, 978-750-8400, fax 978-646-8700. Requests to the Publisher for permission should be addressed to the Legal Department, Wiley Publishing, Inc., 10475 Crosspoint Blvd., Indianapolis, IN 46256, 317-572-3447, fax 317-572-4447, or e-mail permcoordinator@wiley.com

LIMIT OF LIABILITY/DISCLAIMER OF WARRANTY: THE PUBLISHER AND AUTHOR HAVE USED THEIR BEST EFFORTS IN PREPARING THIS BOOK. THE PUBLISHER AND AUTHOR MAKE NO REPRESENTATIONS OR WARRANTIES WITH RESPECT TO THE ACCURACY OR COMPLETENESS OF THE CONTENTS OF THIS BOOK AND SPECIFICALLY DISCLAIM ANY IMPLIED WARRANTIES OF MERCHANTABILITY OR FITNESS FOR A PARTICULAR PURPOSE. THERE ARE NO WARRANTIES WHICH EXTEND BEYOND THE DESCRIPTIONS CONTAINED IN THIS PARAGRAPH. NO WARRANTY MAY BE CREATED OR EXTENDED BY SALES REPRESENTATIVES OR WRITTEN SALES MATERIALS. THE ACCURACY AND COMPLETENESS OF THE INFORMATION PROVIDED HEREIN AND THE OPINIONS STATED HEREIN ARE NOT GUARANTEED OR WARRANTED TO PRODUCE ANY PARTICULAR RESULTS, AND THE ADVICE AND STRATEGIES CONTAINED HEREIN MAY NOT BE SUITABLE FOR EVERY INDIVIDUAL. NEITHER THE PUBLISHER NOR AUTHOR SHALL BE LIABLE FOR ANY LOSS OF PROFIT OR ANY OTHER COMMERCIAL DAMAGES, INCLUDING BUT NOT LIMITED TO SPECIAL, INCIDENTAL, CONSEQUENTIAL, OR OTHER DAMAGES. FULFILLMENT OF EACH COUPON OFFER IS THE RESPONSIBILITY OF THE OFFEROR.

Trademarks: Wiley, the Wiley Publishing logo, Cliffs, CliffsNotes, CliffsAP, CliffsComplete, CliffsTestPrep, CliffsQuickReview, CliffsNote-a-Day, and all related trademarks, logos and trade dress are trademarks or registered trademarks of Wiley Publishing, Inc., in the United States and other countries and may not be used without written permission. All other trademarks are the property of their respective owners. Wiley Publishing, Inc. is not associated with any product or vendor mentioned in this book.

For general information on our other products and services or to obtain technical support, please contact our Customer Care Department within the U.S. at 800-762-2974, outside the U.S. at 317-572-3993, or fax 317-572-4002.

Wiley also published its books in a variety of electronic formats. Some content that appears in print may not be available in electronic books.

Ⓦ WILEY is a trademark of Wiley Publishing, Inc.

Table of Contents

How to Use This Book

CliffsNotes *Dubliners* supplements the original work, giving you background information about the author, an introduction to the novel, a graphical character map, critical commentaries, expanded glossaries, and a comprehensive index. CliffsNotes Review tests your comprehension of the original text and reinforces learning with questions and answers, practice projects, and more. For further information on James Joyce and *Dubliners,* check out the CliffsNotes Resource Center.

CliffsNotes provides the following icons to highlight essential elements of particular interest:

Reveals the underlying themes in the work.

Helps you to more easily relate to or discover the depth of a character.

Uncovers elements such as setting, atmosphere, mystery, passion, violence, irony, symbolism, tragedy, foreshadowing, and satire.

Enables you to appreciate the nuances of words and phrases.

Don't Miss Our Web Site

Discover classic literature as well as modern-day treasures by visiting the CliffsNotes Web site at www.cliffsnotes.com. You can obtain a quick download of a CliffsNotes title, purchase a title in print form, browse our catalog, or view online samples.

You'll also find interactive tools that are fun and informative, links to interesting Web sites, tips, articles, and additional resources to help you. See you at www.cliffsnotes.com!

LIFE AND BACKGROUND OF THE AUTHOR

Formative Years and Education

James Augustine Joyce was born on February 2, 1882, in Dublin, Ireland. At the age of six and a half, he was enrolled at Clongowes Wood College, a Jesuit School for Boys in Ireland's County Kildare. Eventually his family withdrew him from Clongowes, lacking the tuition. From 1893 to 1898 Joyce studied at Belvedere College, another private boys' school, and in 1898 he enrolled at University College, Dublin. He graduated in 1902 with a degree in modern languages. During 1903 he studied medicine in Paris and published reviews; receiving a telegram saying that his mother was deathly ill, he returned to Dublin in time for her death. The following year he met Nora Barnacle, a country girl from the west of Ireland who would become his lifelong companion; their first date took place on June 16, 1904: the day on which Joyce's masterpiece, *Ulysses,* would be set.

Literary Writing

Also in 1904, while teaching school in Ireland, Joyce published stories in *The Irish Homestead* and began a novel, *Stephen Hero,* that would eventually metamorphose into *A Portrait of the Artist As a Young Man.* Though unmarried to Nora Barnacle, he left Ireland with her and they traveled together to Europe, where he taught languages in the Berlitz School in Yugoslavia and then in Trieste, Italy, where their son Giorgio was born. In 1906 Joyce, Nora, and Giorgio moved to Rome, where he worked in a bank, and the following year his collected poems, called *Chamber Music,* were published in London. Also during this time, his daughter Lucia was born.

In 1909 Joyce visited Ireland, where he opened a movie theater in Dublin with the help of some European investors; he also signed a contract for the publication of *Dubliners.* In 1912 he visited Ireland again, this time with his family; the book would not be published until two years later, in London. Also in 1914, Joyce's first completed novel, *A Portrait of the Artist As a Young Man,* was serialized in the London magazine *The Egoist.* He began writing *Ulysses* at this time.

The Joyces moved in 1915 to Switzerland. The following year, *A Portrait* was published in New York. In 1918, his poorly received play, *Exiles,* was published in London. It was also that year that chapters from *Ulysses,* his novel-in-progress, began to appear in the American journal *The Little Review.* Publication of the completed book would not occur until 1922. Ernest Hemingway and Winston Churchill were two of the first to buy the already famous new book.

The writer's *Pomes Pennyeach* was published in 1927; four years later, Joyce and Nora were married in London, already having lived together for over a quarter of a century. In 1933, a New York judge ruled that *Ulysses* was not pornographic; until that time, it had been banned in the United States as obscene. A year later, Random House published the novel, and five years after that, in 1939, *Finnegans Wake* appeared.

Joyce died at the age of 59 on January 13, 1941, in Zurich, where he was buried.

Honors and Awards

Though easily one of the most innovative and influential writers of the twentieth century, James Joyce was little rewarded during his lifetime for his achievements in literature. Upon the appearance of his first published stories, he received the kudos of his literary peers, giants like W.B. Yeats and Ezra Pound. With the publication of *Ulysses* in Paris— and its subsequent banning in the United States and other countries— he achieved worldwide fame and notoriety, appearing, for instance, on the cover of *Time* magazine. Formal recognition, in the form of honors and awards, was scant, however. Amazingly, he never received the Nobel Prize for Literature. Money was rarely forthcoming.

Unlike most other authors, whose status ebbs and flows, Joyce has never gone out of fashion. (In that way he is like his heroes, Shakespeare and Ibsen.) Stylistically, his influence can be seen in the work of literary giants who followed him, ranging from Ernest Hemingway and William Faulkner to Ralph Ellison and Henry Roth. To many writers, scholars, and general readers, he is the very embodiment of the Modern in literature.

James Joyce continues to influence all writers at every level who strive to write about the ordinary, to tell the story of the little guy (or gal). In 1999 a panel convened by the Modern Library named *Ulysses* the most notable novel of the century, with *A Portrait of the Artist As a Young Man* coming in third.

INTRODUCTION
TO THE BOOK

Introduction

Like many important artistic works of the early twentieth century (the paintings of Joyce's contemporary Wassily Kandinsky, for instance, or Louis Armstrong's music), *Dubliners* appears deceptively simple and direct at first, especially compared with James Joyce's later works of fiction: *A Portrait of the Artist As a Young Man, Ulysses,* and *Finnegans Wake.* It is certainly his most *accessible* book—relatively easy to comprehend and follow, whereas the others mentioned tend to challenge even the most sophisticated reader.

It was in *Dubliners* that Joyce developed his storytelling muscles, honing the nuts-and-bolts craftsmanship that would make the high modern art of *A Portrait of the Artist As a Young Man, Ulysses,* and *Finnegans Wake* viable. In *Dubliners,* he does not yet employ the techniques of mimetic narrative (characteristic of *A Portrait*) or stream-of-consciousness *(Ulysses),* but he paves the way here for those technical breakthroughs. *Dubliners* is somewhat comparable to Picasso's so-called Rose and Blue periods, in which the painter perfected his skills at realistic portrayal with paint before pioneering cubism and other abstract styles. Joyce even introduces characters (Lenehan from "Two Gallants" and Bob Doran from "The Boarding House," for instance) who reappear in his later books.

Mainly, Joyce worked and played in *Dubliners* at plotting and characterization, description and dialogue, and (especially) point of view (the technical term for who is telling a story, to whom, and with what limitations). What is amazing is that such a relatively immature work succeeds almost without exception. And just as Picasso's realist works have not only lasted but are actually preferred by many museum goers to his more difficult-to-appreciate later paintings, *Dubliners* is the favorite James Joyce book of many readers.

The setting of *Dubliners* is, logically enough, in and around the city of Dublin, Ireland. Though the capital city of Ireland, the Dublin in which Joyce grew up was a provincial place—far less cosmopolitan than a number of other Western European cities of similar size (Venice, for instance). Unlike France, Spain, and Italy, Ireland had never been a center of continental culture; unlike England and the Netherlands, it had never been a trade hub. Nor, in contrast to then recently united Germany, was Ireland yet industrialized. (In fact, the country would remain almost exclusively rural for decades to come.) It was a kind of third-world nation, really, before the term existed. Though Dublin was a genuinely urban locale, with electric lights and streetcars, competing daily newspapers and even a museum, the city remained fairly unsophisticated at the time when Joyce wrote about it.

To some degree, this was a function of Ireland's geographical remoteness from the rest of the continent in the days before radio and air travel (much less television and the Internet). It is an island off an island (Britain) off the coast of Europe, and therefore somewhat inaccessible. James Joyce himself, however, blamed two other factors for the backwardness of his home city: the Roman Catholic Church and the neighboring country of England.

According to legend, St. Patrick had brought Christianity to Ireland in the Middle Ages; ever since, most Irish have observed a rigorous and rather literal brand of the religion, one that is perhaps more superstitious than the Christianity practiced by French Catholics, for instance. In story after story in *Dubliners* as well as in the novels he wrote later in his career, Joyce holds the Roman Catholic Church accountable for the failure of the Irish to advance in step with the rest of Europe. He was particularly bitter about the way in which the Church often recruited intellectuals like himself to serve in the priesthood—rather than encouraging them to use their minds in the service of progress, as doctors, scientists, or engineers.

Joyce also blamed England for what he saw as Ireland's backwardness. On July 1, 1690, at the Battle of the Boyne, the Protestant forces of King William III of England had defeated the Roman Catholic Jacobites of James II, causing the downfall of Catholic Ireland. Until 1922, when British Parliament granted independence to the country (while retaining control of what is to this day the province of Northern Ireland, the inhabitants of which tend to be Protestant rather than Catholic), Joyce's homeland would remain, in effect, a colony of England. Joyce and many other Irish saw this era of over 200 years as one of outright occupation by an overtly hostile enemy.

The period during which *Dubliners* is set follows the brutal so-called Potato Famine of the late 1840s—for which many Irish held the British responsible—after which a movement for Irish independence (led by the nationalist Charles Stewart Parnell) occurred. This movement, however, failed ignominiously when Parnell was betrayed by his own countrymen, and in the Dublin of Joyce's novels, the defeat still stings. (For evidence of this, see "Ivy Day in the Committee Room.") The Irish

Revival, a movement begun in the 1880s to foster understanding and respect for Celtic and Gaelic language and culture, is referred to in *Dubliners* as well (in "A Mother" and "The Dead"). From the very first story onward, the book is rife with examples, obvious and less so, of the treachery of England and the English, at least in the opinion of Joyce and his characters.

The stories of *Dubliners* are united by the city itself—Dublin is rendered in Joyce's book with a concreteness and specificity that was unprecedented at the time of its writing. The other aspect that unites these disparate works of narrative prose is shared *themes*. Though the protagonist of "Araby" and that of "Clay" could hardly be more different with respect to age and temperament (the same goes for the main characters of "Eveline" and "The Dead"), all these stories are united by the *ideas* that the tales dramatize: *paralysis, corruption,* and *death.* In story after *Dubliners* story, characters fail to move forward, tending rather to forge outward and then retreat, or else circle endlessly. They are stuck in place. Examples of corruption—that is, contamination, deterioration, perversity, and depravity—occur throughout. Finally, *Dubliners* begins with a death and ends with a death (in a story titled, logically enough, "The Dead"), with numerous deaths either dramatized or referred to in between.

All of this knits the book's many and varied stories together in a web of place, time, and meaning. Each successive story gains in momentum and weight by virtue of following those that came before. (For instance, Gabriel Conroy from "The Dead" is more completely understood if thought of as the grown-up protagonist of "Araby.") And after reading the book, it will be hard to think of one *Dubliners* tale without remembering others.

CRITICAL COMMENTARIES: *DUBLINERS*

The Sisters

Summary

It is 1895 in Dublin, Ireland when an **unnamed boy** comes down to supper one evening. Family friend **Old Cotter** is telling **the boy's aunt and uncle** that the boy's mentor, **Father James Flynn,** has passed away after a third stroke. The two men share the opinion that spending time with Father Flynn was unhealthy for the boy, who should have been playing "with young lads of his own age." In bed later, the boy tries to understand why Old Cotter and his uncle would not want him to associate with Father Flynn; then he imagines or dreams about the priest trying to confess something to him.

The following morning, the boy visits Father Flynn's house and finds a card displayed outside announcing the man's death, but he does not knock on the door. He feels less sad than he would have expected; in fact, the boy experiences "a sensation of freedom" as a result of his mentor's death. That evening, the boy's aunt takes him on a formal visit to the house of mourning. He sees the body of Father Flynn lying in an open casket, after which the boy's aunt and **the priest's two sisters** converse cryptically about the deceased, implying that he was mentally unstable for some time before dying and that he may have been involved in some scandal or other.

Commentary

This, the first story in *Dubliners,* introduces many of the themes and motifs that will recur throughout the book, linking its component parts together into something that is not quite a novel but more than a mere collection of short stories.

The first theme is *paralysis.* James Joyce believed that the Irish society and culture, as well as the country's economy, had been paralyzed for centuries by two forces. The first was the Roman Catholic Church, the teachings of which most Dubliners of Joyce's day adhered to passionately. The second was England, which had conquered Ireland in the seventeenth century and resisted granting the country its independence until 1922.

In the first line of "Sisters," Father Flynn has suffered a third and fatal stroke—a malfunctioning of blood vessels in the brain that can cause paralysis, if not death. In fact, it may have been a stroke that resulted in the scandalous dropping of the chalice revealed near the end of the story. And of course, the gray face in the boy's dream that "had died of paralysis" is that of Father Flynn himself.

Clearly Father Flynn represents the paralyzed Catholic Church in this story—and the church's ability to paralyze others. The time spent with the priest prevents the boy from having fun with his peers. Father Flynn, in turn, lives on Great Britain Street and dies on the anniversary of England's victory over Ireland in 1690.

The second theme that Joyce introduces is *corruption.* In the second paragraph of this story, the narrator (storyteller) mentions the word *simony,* the selling of blessings, pardons, or other favors by the Roman Catholic Church to its members. Later, Father Flynn will be referred to as a *simoniac,* one guilty of this offense. Because corruption prevents progress, it is closely related to the theme of paralysis.

The third theme is *death,* whether that death be physical or merely spiritual. Joyce's attitude toward death is complex. In "The Sisters," for example, physical death is not entirely bad, as it frees Father Flynn from what sounds like a miserable life. Indeed, the last image of the priest shows him "sitting in the dark in his confession box, wide-awake and laughing-like softly to himself." The priest's death liberates the boy, too—from the paralysis, corruption, and death that Joyce clearly felt would come to him if his association with the church continued. "I found it strange," the narrator says, "that neither I nor the day seemed in a mourning mood and I felt even annoyed at discovering in myself a sensation of freedom as if I had been freed from something by his death." On the other hand, Father Flynn seems to have been suffering a kind of spiritual death long before he actually passed away. (Note: *Dubliners* not only begins with a death, it ends with one, too—the remembered death of Michael Furey, in "The Dead.")

Finally, notice Father Flynn's "big discoloured teeth"—yellow or brown, presumably. Yellow and brown are the colors symbolic of decay and paralysis throughout the work of James Joyce. Much more of this color scheme is to be found in the other stories of *Dubliners.*

Glossary

(Here and in the following stories, difficult words and phrases, as well as allusions and historical references, are explained.)

gnomon   a column or pin on a sundial that casts a shadow indicating the time of day.

simony   the buying or selling of sacred or spiritual things, as sacraments or benefices. Roman Catholic teaching defines simony as an infringement of natural law.

stirabout   porridge.

faint   the crude, impure spirits given off in the first and last stages the distillation of liquor.

worm   the coil of a still.

Rosicrucian   any of a number of persons in the seventeenth or eighteenth century who professed to be members of a secret society said to have various sorts of occult lore and power. The boy's uncle is implying that his relationship with Father Flynn was secret and possibly dangerous.

Drapery   a shop selling cloth.

July 1st   the date, in 1690, of the Battle of the Boyne, in which the Protestant forces of William III of England defeated the Roman Catholic Jacobites of James III, resulting in the downfall of Catholic Ireland.

High Toast   a brand of snuff.

catacombs   any of a series of vaults or galleries in an underground burial place. During the first and second century, persecuted Christians hid in the catacombs beneath Rome.

venial   not causing spiritual death; said of a sin either not serious in itself or, if serious, not adequately recognized as such or not committed with full consent of one's will.

And everything . . . ?   apparently the boy's aunt seeks to establish that last rites were bestowed upon Father Flynn by a priest before death; only a profoundly disgraced priest would be refused last rites, so the fact that she has to ask implies much about Father Flynn's misbehavior.

breviary   a book containing the Psalms, readings, prayers, and so on of the Divine Office.

rheumatic wheels   a malapropism for pneumatic wheels.

An Encounter

Summary

As in "The Sisters," an **unnamed storyteller** (possibly the same narrator featured in that story) recalls a transformative boyhood experience. Here, the boy schemes with his friends **Leo Dillon** and **Mahony** to play hooky from their exclusive private school one day in June and walk across Dublin, and then ride a ferry boat across the River Liffey to the Pigeon House. When Dillon fails to show up, the narrator and Mahony leave without him.

After crossing the Liffey, the boys chase a stray cat across a field and encounter **a stranger** there. The man quizzes the narrator and Mahony on the books they've read, and then asks them if they have girlfriends. After a while, the man crosses the field and does something that the boys find "queer"—probably masturbating. Then he returns. When Mahony leaves to pursue the cat further, the strange man talks obsessively to the protagonist (main character) about the need for boys who misbehave to be whipped. When the stranger is done talking, the boy leaves, seeking Mahony.

Commentary

Theme

Joyce continues here the themes of paralysis and spiritual death begun in "The Sisters." This story's main character wants more than to play cowboys and Indians with his schoolmates; he wants "real adventures." But he knows that "real adventures . . . do not happen to people who remain at home: they must be sought abroad." Thus, he skips school one day and sets out for the Pigeon House across Dublin with his friend Mahony.

Literary Device

Significantly, however, the two truants never reach their destination. Instead, they are waylaid by a pervert with green eyes—Ireland's nickname is the Emerald Isle—who becomes sexually excited when the boys discuss girlfriends, though it appears he is more aroused by the boys themselves than by the young girls they mention. At this point the stranger walks away to masturbate, a kind of paralysis because it is sex that does not result in procreation. After his return, the man becomes aroused again while talking about whips and whipping.

Although neither of the boys has been overtly harmed by the incident, their journey in search of adventure has ended unexpectedly, to say the least, in an encounter (their first, probably) with adult sexuality and the kind of spiritual death represented in "The Sisters" by Father Flynn. Note that both old men show yellow teeth when they smile; the colors yellow and brown are symbolic of decay and paralysis throughout Joyce's work. Ireland itself has foiled their attempt at discovery and development.

Glossary

numbers   issues.

tea-cosy   a knitted or padded cover placed over a teapot to keep the contents hot.

hearing the four pages of Roman History   supervising a class in Latin translation.

michin   (slang) playing hooky.

coping   the top layer of a masonry wall, usually sloped to carry off water.

pipeclayed   whitened with pipe clay, a white, plastic clay used for making clay tobacco pipes or pottery; possibly a foreshadowing of "Clay," a later Dubliners story.

mall   a street on the south side of Dublin's Royal Canal.

air   a song or tune.

to have some gas with   (slang) to have fun with.

Vitriol Works   a north Dublin chemical factory.

Swaddlers! Swaddlers!   Dublin slang for Protestants.

cricket   a game associated by the Irish with the English conquest of their country.

Smoothing Iron   a bathing place on Dublin Bay's north side.

right skit   (slang) great fun.

jerry hat   a stiff felt hat.

totties   (slang) girlfriends.

josser   (slang) fellow; guy.

Araby

Summary

A young boy who is similar in age and temperament to those in "The Sisters" and "An Encounter" develops a crush on **Mangan's sister,** a girl who lives across the street. One evening she asks him if he plans to go to a bazaar (a fair organized, probably by a church, to raise money for charity) called Araby. The girl will be away on a retreat when the bazaar is held and therefore unable to attend. The boy promises that if he goes he will bring her something from Araby.

The boy requests and receives permission to attend the bazaar on Saturday night. When Saturday night comes, however, his **uncle** returns home late, possibly having visited a pub after work. After much anguished waiting, the boy receives money for the bazaar, but by the time he arrives at Araby, it is too late. The event is shutting down for the night, and he does not have enough money to buy something nice for Mangan's sister anyway. The boy cries in frustration.

Commentary

Like the two previous stories, "The Sisters" and "An Encounter," "Araby" is about a somewhat introverted boy fumbling toward adulthood with little in the way of guidance from family or community. The truants in "An Encounter" managed to play hooky from school without any major consequences; no one prevented them from journeying across town on a weekday or even asked the boys where they were going. Similarly, the young protagonist of this story leaves his house after nine o'clock at night, when "people are in bed and after their first sleep," and travels through the city in darkness with the assent of his guardians. Like the main character in "The Sisters," this boy lives not with his parents but with an aunt and uncle, the latter of whom is certainly good-natured but seems to have a drinking problem. When the man returns home, he is talking to himself and he almost knocks over the coat rack. He has forgotten about his promise to the boy, and when reminded of it—twice—he becomes distracted by the connection between the name of the bazaar and the title of a poem he knows. The boy's aunt is so passive that her presence proves inconsequential.

Like "An Encounter," "Araby" takes the form of a quest—a journey in search of something precious or even sacred. Once again, the quest is ultimately in vain. In "An Encounter," the Pigeon House was the object of the search; here, it is Araby. Note the sense of something passionately sought, against the odds: "We walked through the flaring streets, jostled by drunken men and bargaining women, amid the curses of labourers, the shrill litanies of shop-boys who stood on guard by the barrels of pigs' cheeks, the nasal chanting of street-singers. . . . These noises converged in a single sensation of life for me: I imagined that I bore my chalice safely through a throng of foes."

Theme

Although the boy ultimately reaches the bazaar, he arrives too late to buy Mangan's sister a decent gift there, and thus he may as well have stayed home: paralysis. Like the narrator of "An Encounter," this protagonist knows that "real adventures . . . must be sought abroad." And yet, having set his sights on something exotic or at least exotic sounding ("Araby" means Arabia, and the bazaar features a French-style café), the boy cannot get there in time for his experience to be worth anything. Why? Because his uncle, who holds the money that will make the excursion possible, has been out drinking.

Some critics have suggested that Mangan's sister represents Ireland itself, and that therefore the boy's quest is made on behalf of his native country. Certainly, the bazaar seems to combine elements of the Catholic Church and England (the two entities that Joyce blamed most for his country's paralysis), just as Father Flynn's death did in "The Sisters." As the church has hypnotized its adherents, Araby has "cast an Eastern enchantment" over the boy. Moreover, it is "not some Freemason [Protestant] affair." Church parishes often organized bazaars to raise money for charity. When the boy reaches the object of his quest, however, Araby (the church) is empty—except for a woman and two men who speak with English accents. The woman speaks to the story's main character in a manner that is "not encouraging" and is clearly doing so "out of a sense of duty."

Thus, a mission on behalf of an idealized homeland (the boy does not actually *know* Mangan's sister—she is more or less a fantasy to him) is thwarted in turn by the Irish themselves (the charming uncle and his propensity to drink), the church, and England.

Style & Language

In addition to being an artist of the highest order, Joyce was also a consummate craftsman. He guides his readers through the story itself, thereby seducing them into considering his themes. First, he offers a main character who elicits sympathy because of his sensitivity and loneliness. Joyce then provides that protagonist with a specific, dramatic conflict (the need to impress Mangan's sister with a gift from Araby). Though apparently minor, this desire is compelling because it is so intensely felt by him. He cares, so the reader cares.

Then the writer puts roadblocks in the way of the boy and the reader: the wait for Saturday itself, and then for the uncle's return from work. Joyce expands time, stretches it out, by piling on the trivial details that torture the boy as he waits: the ticking of the clock, the cries of the protagonist's playmates outside, the gossiping of Mrs. Mercer, the scratching of the uncle's key in the lock, and the rocking of the hallstand. Then the uncle must eat dinner and be reminded twice of Araby, after which begins the agonizingly slow journey itself, which seems to take place in slow motion, like a nightmare. When the protagonist finally arrives at the bazaar, too late, the reader wants so badly for the boy to buy something, anything, for Mangan's sister that when he says "No, thank you" to the Englishwoman who speaks to him, it is heartbreaking. "Gazing up into the darkness," the narrator says, "I saw myself as a creature driven and derided by vanity; and my eyes burned with anguish and anger." The eyes of Joyce's readers burn, too, as they read this.

One final point: Though all are written from the first-person *point-of-view*, or perspective, in none of the first three stories in *Dubliners* is the young protagonist himself telling the story, exactly. It is instead the grown-up version of each boy who recounts "The Sisters," "An Encounter," and "Araby." This is shown by the language used and the insights included in these stories. A young boy would never have the wisdom or the vocabulary to say "I saw myself as a creature driven and derided by vanity." The man that the boy grew into, however, is fully capable of recognizing and expressing such a sentiment. Joyce's point-of-view strategy thereby allows the reader to examine the feelings of his young protagonists while experiencing those feelings in all their immediate, overwhelming pain.

Glossary

blind   a dead-end; A dead-end features prominently in "Two Gallants," as well.

areas   spaces providing light and air to the basements of houses.

O'Donovan Rossa   Jeremiah O'Donovan (1831–1915), nicknamed Dynamite Rossa; an Irish revolutionary.

the troubles   a euphemism for Irish civil unrest.

Freemason   an international secret society having as its principles brotherliness, charity, and mutual aid. Many Dublin Roman Catholics were hostile to Freemasons, who were generally Protestants.

collected used stamps for some pious purpose   selling used postage stamps to collectors to raise money for charity.

The Arab's Farewell to His Steed   a poem by Irish poet Caroline Norton (1808–77).

Eveline

Summary

Eveline Hill, a 19-year-old woman who works in a Dublin shop, sits inside her family's house recalling childhood, including some happy memories as well as her **father's** drunken brutality to her and her siblings. Eveline thinks about people she has known who have either left Ireland (a priest who has traveled to Melbourne, for example) or died (her mother and her brother Ernest), and of her own plans to leave the country with a man named **Frank.** She recalls meeting Frank, an Irish sailor now living in Argentina, and dating him while he visited Dublin on vacation. Eveline also thinks about her father's disapproval of Frank, and of her promise "to keep the home together as long as she could" before her mother grew deranged and died. Later, gripped by fear of the unknown and probably guilt as well, Eveline finds herself unable to board the ferry to England, where she and Frank are scheduled to meet a ship bound for South America. He leaves without her.

Commentary

Theme

Though short and easy to read, this story is devastating, possibly the most powerful in the book. (The other candidate for that honor would be "The Dead.") It is yet another *Dubliners* tale about paralysis, as Eveline stands on the pier at story's end, frozen in place by fear and guilt. She wants to leave Ireland, but she quite literally cannot move, speak, or even express emotion on her face. A crippled childhood friend called Little Keogh, whom Eveline recalls early in the story, perhaps foreshadows her own eventual paralysis.

Death pervades "Eveline" too: the deaths of her mother and her brother Ernest, and of a girlhood friend named Tizzie Dunn. And of course, Eveline fears her own death: "he would drown her," she thinks of Frank, defying logic. Perhaps she unconsciously associates her fiancé with the other man in her life, her brutal father.

As usual, Joyce holds the Catholic Church and England account-able, albeit subtly. Though Eveline's father's cry of "Damned Italians! coming over here!" is of course irrational, it reminds the reader of the seat of the church's power in Rome, and the way that power affects even distant Ireland. Note that Eveline's dockside paralysis is preceded by a prayer "to God to direct her, to show her what was her duty"—and that a bell (like a church bell) clangs "upon her heart" as Frank grasps her hand in vain at story's end. Also, be aware that like contemporary air-line passengers flying first to a hub airport before boarding planes for their final destinations, Irish travelers for South America at the turn of the twentieth century had to travel first by ferry to Liverpool, England. Neighbors named the Waters have "gone back to England," but Eveline is incapable of straying even that far from home, much less across the Atlantic.

Theme

Thus, this is the third *Dubliners* story in a row about a failed quest. The Holy Grail of the boy in "An Encounter" was the Pigeon House, which he never reached; the main character in "Araby" sought the bazaar, closing down by the time he got there. Eveline seeks Argentina, a place where she hopes to avoid the very real threat of her father's violence as well as her dead mother's "life of commonplace sacrifices closing in final craziness." "People would treat her with respect," Eveline thinks of married life in Argentina.

She believes she has a right to happiness, too—that is, until she stands on the shore and confronts the reality of the journey on which she is about to embark. Then fear and guilt (about abandoning her father and her younger siblings) overwhelm her, and she stays rather than goes. Though it is as old and dusty as her father's house ("She looked round the room, reviewing all its familiar objects which she had dusted once a week for so many years, wondering where on earth all the dust came from"), Dublin is at least familiar, and Eveline is a fear-ful young woman, obsessed with thoughts of wild Patagonians and remembered ghost stories. "He rushed beyond the barrier and called to her to follow," the tale concludes. "He was shouted at to go on but he still called to her. She set her white face to him, passive, like a helpless animal. Her eyes gave him no sign of love or farewell or recognition." Though this is not certain, it seems unlikely that Eveline will ever leave home now. Frank seems to have been her last, best chance.

Glossary

cretonne   a heavy, unglazed, printed cotton or linen cloth; used for curtains, slipcovers, and so on.

blackthorn stick   a cane or stick made from the stem of the blackthorn, a thorny, white-flowered prunus shrub with purple or black plumlike fruit.

nix   (slang) silent.

Blessed Margaret Mary Alacoque   (1647–90) a French nun beatified in 1864 and canonized in 1920.

Stores   the shop where Eveline works.

night-boat   the ferry that departed Dublin every evening for Liverpool, England.

The Bohemian Girl   a popular nineteenth-century light opera composed by Dublin musician Michael William Balfe. Characters throughout *Dubliners* refer to songs from this opera.

Patagonians   inhabitants of Patagonia, a dry, grassy region in south South America, east of the Andes (including the south parts of Argentina and Chile); thought to be nomadic and dangerous.

Derevaun Seraun! Derevaun Seraun!   probably gibberish.

After the Race

Summary

After an automobile race outside Dublin, a 26-year-old Irishman named **Jimmy,** the son of a wealthy former butcher, accompanies the French team back into the city. Jimmy was educated at a Catholic preparatory school in England, then Trinity College in Dublin, and finally at Cambridge University (though he was never a serious student). Back in Dublin, Jimmy and one of the drivers **(Villona)** change their clothes at his parents' house, and then join the others **(Ségouin** and **Rivière)** as well as a young Englishman (Routh) for dinner at the hotel of a team member. Afterward, accompanied by an American **(Farley),** Jimmy, the French racing team, and the Englishman take a train to nearby Kingstown. There they board the American's yacht. Aboard the yacht they dance, eat, drink, and play cards, at which Jimmy loses a great deal of money.

Commentary

Unlike most of the other stories in *Dubliners,* "After the Race" is not highly regarded by most critics, who believe that Joyce was describing here a social class (the very wealthy) about which he knew very little.

Still, it is consistent with the other stories in the collection with regard to both theme and symbolism. Jimmy illustrates the theme of *paralysis* by not progressing in any real way. Jimmy's parents have used the money earned by his father in the butcher trade to send him to a series of highly regarded schools, and yet Jimmy seems to have learned very little as a result of his lavish education. Sure, he has made friends (like Charles Segouin, the owner of the racing car and a proprietor-to-be of an automobile dealership in Paris), but those friends are not necessarily loyal to Jimmy. From the opening scene, in which Jimmy cannot hear the driver and his cousin in the front seat over the Hungarian Villona's humming and the noise of the car itself, the reader has a sense of Jimmy's half-baked membership in the group. In fact, the team probably tolerates Jimmy strictly because of the money (his father's) that he has promised to invest in Segouin's company.

A racing car goes nowhere, of course, and though Jimmy boards a yacht near the story's conclusion, the boat remains at anchor—paralyzed. He feels as though he is accomplishing much on the night after the race, but like Dublin itself, which "wore the mask of a capital" though not really a capital, Jimmy's accomplishments are an illusion. In fact, he is worse off at the end of "After the Race" than he was at the beginning, having lost all his money at cards. Because it was this money that made him acceptable to the team in the first place, his flirtation with Continental glamour is probably near its end.

Literary Device

The French driver has "a line of shining white teeth" in contrast to the yellow or brown teeth seen on Irish characters to date (yellow and brown being Joyce's colors of decay and paralysis). Also, Jimmy's luck begins to change when the Englishman, Routh, joins the group; Jimmy himself was educated in England and at Protestant, Anglocentric Trinity College in Dublin. As in earlier stories, Joyce blames the English for Irish paralysis when he can.

Glossary

their friends, the French   the Irish identified with the French, traditionally rivals of the English, if not their enemies.

advanced Nationalist   a supporter of the Irish Parliamentary Party, which sought independence for the country.

the Bank   the Bank of Ireland; originally the Irish Parliament Building.

the mask of a capital   though Dublin was a provincial capital, it had wielded no actual power over Ireland since the Act of Union was passed in 1801.

"Cadet Roussel"   (French) a song from the 1790s.

"Ho! Ho! Hohé, vraiment!"   the refrain from "Cadet Rousel."

Two Gallants

Summary

On a Sunday evening in August, a young man named **Corley** has told another, **Lenehan**, of a plan he has hatched with **a housekeeper** engaged in prostitution on the side. Corley goes off with the young woman, while Lenehan walks idly around Dublin until 10:30, stopping only to eat a dinner of peas and ginger beer at a pub. Finally, exactly according to plan, Lenehan observes from a distance but does not interrupt as the woman enters via the basement the elegant house where she works and emerges from the front door. Minutes later, Corley shows Lenehan what she has stolen from inside: a gold coin.

Commentary

Literary Device

In this story, Joyce reiterates the motif of a circular path that leads nowhere, introduced by implication in "After the Race." The author is even more compulsive than usual at including actual Dublin place names in "Two Gallants"—to a fault, perhaps. He does so partly to stress the story's veracity. These events could really happen, Joyce is telling us—maybe they did! But he also does this so that readers familiar with the city's geography would recognize that Lenehan, who will reappear in Joyce's novel *Ulysses,* ends his evening's odyssey not far from where he began it. Like Jimmy in "After the Race," Eveline (in the story of the same name), and the protagonist of "An Encounter," Lenehan has ventured out only to return to the place where he began. Clearly, the three frustrated characters who preceded him are going home after their stories conclude.

In keeping with a common theme in *Dubliners,* "Two Gallants" lays blame with the Catholic Church for Irish paralysis: The blue-and-white of the slavey's outfit recalls the Virgin Mary's traditional colors. But England is especially responsible here; almost every place name referenced on Lenehan's pointless roundabout, from Rutland Square (named for an English politician) to the neighborhood near (Protestant) Trinity College and City Hall, was associated by Irish-Catholic Dubliners with the English.

The street on which "Two Gallants" concludes is a dead end. Obviously Corley (a kind of poor man's criminal mastermind) and the slavey (a thief, by story's end) are already dead, in a spiritual sense. Lenehan, killing time on a warm summer evening merely so that he can witness a petty crime, is not far behind.

Literary Device

Finally, symbolism in this story is fairly straightforward, though sometimes ironical. The harp is a time-honored emblem of Ireland and means precisely what it appears to. The double halo around the moon, however, appears here as a reminder that neither Lenehan nor Corley is a saint, and that the woman in blue and white is no virgin. Joyce's private symbolic system (using the colors of yellow and brown to indicate decay) takes over at the end of "Two Gallants"—the coin the young woman steals is yellow in color.

Glossary

public-house   a pub; a bar or tavern.

slavey   (British informal) a female domestic servant, especially one who does hard, menial work.

up to the dodge   (slang) capable of avoiding pregnancy.

hairy   (slang) cunning.

about town   a euphemism for unemployed.

hard word   unpleasant information (that employment might be available for Corley, who doesn't like to work).

he aspirated the first letter of his name in the manner of the Florentines   he pronounced Corley as "whorely."

on the turf   (slang) engaged in prostitution.

get inside me   (slang) take my place.

the chains   chains that used to separate paths around Stephen's Green from the streets beyond.

Half ten   10:30.

a little of the ready   (slang) with money available.

the area of a house   a space providing light and air to the basement of a house.

The Boarding House

Summary

Mrs. Mooney, who has been separated from her abusive alcoholic husband ever since he tried to kill her with a cleaver, runs a boarding house occupied by music-hall performers, tourists, and a number of young Dublin clerks. Her daughter, Polly, worked briefly as a typist and now labors as a housekeeper at home. When Polly becomes involved with one of the boarders, a clerk in his mid-thirties named Mr. Doran, Mrs. Mooney does not interfere.

Instead, she allows the affair to continue until other lodgers at the house have observed it. Then she insists that Doran marry her daughter. Doran already feels guilty, thanks to a meeting with his priest the night before, and he is worried that his employer will get wind of the affair. Also, he is concerned that Polly might try to "put an end to herself," and he fears the wrath of Polly's brother Jack. Despite the fact that he does not love her, and that his family will look down on the marriage because the Mooneys belong to an inferior social class, Doran agrees to wed Polly.

Commentary

Theme

More paralysis, death, and corruption—and more symbolism and storytelling craftsmanship—are evident in "The Boarding House." As in "An Encounter," "Araby," "Eveline," and "After the Race," a character in "The Boarding House" (Polly) ventures forth—to her typist's job at the corn-factor's—only to return home without having achieved the object of her quest. In Polly's case, the quest is for a life independent of her mother. Though over thirty years old, Mr. Doran (who, like Lenehan, will return as a supporting character in *Ulysses*) seems to have made little forward progress in life, and he will make even less as Mrs. Mooney's son-in-law. Somehow hobbled until now, frozen at present with fear of Jack Mooney, he will be from this day on genuinely paralyzed—as paralyzed as Polly, her mother, and so many *Dubliners* characters before and after them.

Though Mrs. Mooney avoided her husband's meat cleaver, it makes little difference, as she is spiritually dead at the time during which "The

Boarding House" takes place. It is no coincidence that the story's narrator refers to her as "the Madame." Like the proprietress of a whorehouse, she hopes to earn money from the young woman living under her roof and thus gives Polly "the run of the young men" there. (This corrupt financial transaction is reminiscent of Father Flynn's simony in "The Sisters.")

Literary Device

Joyce's private system of color symbolism (yellows and browns indicating decay) is used again in "The Boarding House." The yellows appear in "yellow streaks of eggs," "butter safe under lock and key," "the little gilt clock," and it is a *corn*-factor for whom Polly works. Examples of browns are the "beer or stout," "bacon-fat," "pieces of broken bread," and Jack Mooney's bottles of Bass ale. The Catholic Church's implied guilt in the matter of Irish paralysis is also dramatized: Doran went to confession the night before he agrees to marry Polly, where the priest "so magnified his sin that he was almost thankful at being afforded a loophole of reparation." When he walks downstairs to talk with Mrs. Mooney, Mr. Doran leaves Polly moaning "*O my God!*" on the bed.

Style & Language

Joyce excelled not only at the art of fiction, but (as in "Araby") at the craft of storytelling, too. Much of this tale's drama is lent to it by the fact that Joyce tells it from three different points-of-view, in series: Mrs. Mooney's, Mr. Doran's, and Polly Mooney's. This is the first story in *Dubliners* told from more than one perspective. "The Sisters," "An Encounter," and "Araby" were of course limited to the perspectives of their first-person narrator. "Eveline," "After the Race," and "Two Gallants" are told from the third-person point-of-view, but the reader never knows what anyone beside Eveline, Jimmy, and Lenehan is thinking or feeling. Here, ever so subtly, Joyce expands his canvas, becoming more novelistic—more like the writer of the sprawling, panoramic novel *Ulysses,* at least with respect to point of view.

Glossary

take the pledge   take an oath not to consume alcoholic beverages.

sheriff's man   a revenue and debt collector.

favourites and outsiders   likely and less-likely winners in a horse race.

handy with the mitts   (slang) a good fighter.

corn-factor's   an agent for the sale of corn.

short twelve   noon mass.

sit   (slang) situation.

screw   (British slang) salary.

pier-glass   a tall mirror set in the pier, or section, between windows.

Reynold's Newspaper   a London newspaper that reported on scandalous events.

a certain fame   a bad reputation.

combing-jacket   a bathrobe.

return-room   a room, usually small, added to the wall of a house.

A Little Cloud

Summary

One evening, a fussy, conservative Dublin clerk known as **Little Chandler** sets out to meet his old friend **Gallaher** at a restaurant called Corless's. Gallaher left Dublin eight years earlier and has made a success of himself as a journalist in London. On the way, Little Chandler fantasizes about succeeding himself, as a writer of poetry. At the restaurant, Gallaher tells Little Chandler about his adventures abroad; afterward, Little Chandler returns home to his wife **(Annie)** and baby daughter, where he fantasizes further about success as a poet, loses his temper with the child, and then feels remorseful.

Commentary

Theme

This story reiterates the dynamic of "An Encounter," "Araby," and "Eveline," as Little Chandler sets out seeking Gallaher and all he represents, only to return home defeated. It also resembles "After the Race" in that Little Chandler quests like Jimmy for European sophistication and winds up as provincial as ever. At the same time, parallels exist between Little Chandler/Gallaher and Lenehan/Corley from "Two Gallants." The first member of each set is so misguided that he admires and hopes to emulate the second—though Gallaher, like Corley, is spiritually dead.

A new twist, not seen in other *Dubliners* tales, is the notion that escape from Ireland does not necessarily equal salvation. "If you wanted to succeed you had to get away," Little Chandler thinks, echoing the thoughts of the narrator in "An Encounter" ("real adventures . . . do not happen to people who remain at home: they must be sought abroad"). And yet Gallaher, who got away, has succeeded in only the most superficial sense. Despite having seen London and Paris and heard talk of Berlin, he is shallow, boorish, and alone. "A Little Cloud" is a turning point in the collection, because it implies that, contrary to what so many of the book's characters believe, flight from Ireland is not necessarily the solution to their problems. This was hinted at in "After the Race" (in which, after all, Jimmy has "studied" abroad), but it is truly dramatized here, in the insufferable, obnoxious figure of Gallaher.

Literary Device

Finally, the conclusion of "A Little Cloud," in which Little Chandler returns dissatisfied to his family and shouts at his crying child, will be brutally reiterated in the ending of the next story, "Counterparts." This binds the two stories together, as "The Sisters," "An Encounter," and "Araby" are bound by their interchangeable protagonists. Again, Joyce conceived *Dubliners* as an integral work of fiction, not merely a collection of stories. Techniques such as these lend the volume coherence.

Glossary

got on   (slang) succeeded.

on the London Press   in the world of British journalism.

When his hour had struck   when the work day had ended.

the gaunt spectral mansions in which the old nobility of Dublin had roistered   buildings originally constructed to house the wealthy had deteriorated and were occupied by poor people early in the twentieth century.

Atalanta   a beautiful, swift-footed maiden who offers to marry any man able to defeat her in a race: Hippomenes wins by dropping three golden apples, which she stops to pick up, along the way. The motif of Greek mythology (including the image of the golden apple) will reappear in Gabriel Conroy's speech in "The Dead."

Half time   (slang) time out.

considering cap   an Irish term equivalent to the American term "thinking cap."

across the water   (Irish slang) in England.

Lithia   lithia water, a mineral water containing lithium salts.

Press life   the life of a journalist.

deuced   extremely; very.

Land Commission   the Irish Land Commission Court, a British agency.

sore head and a fur on my tongue   hung over.

Moulin Rouge   literally "Red Windmill," a Parisian music hall.

catholic   all-inclusive.

students' balls   dances in Parisian cafes, especially those on the Left Bank, the location of the University of Paris.

cocottes   (French) literally, hens. Probably used by Galaher to mean prostitutes.

rum   (informal, chiefly British) odd; queer.

palm   prize.

parole d'honneur   (French) word of honor.

an a.p.   (slang) an appointment.

deoc an doruis   (Irish) literally door drink; last round.

put your head in the sack   (slang) apparently, get married.

Bewley's   a chain of coffeehouses.

Hushed are the winds . . .   the first stanza of the poem "On the Death of a Young Lady, Cousin of the Author, and Very Dear to Him" (1802) by George Gordon, Lord Byron (1788–1824), an English poet.

Lambabaun   (Irish) lamb child.

Counterparts

Summary

Humiliated by his boss **(Mr. Alleyne)** at the law firm in which he works, a copy clerk named **Farrington** pawns his watch and spends the money on a night of drinking in Dublin pubs. Afterward, he goes to his house in the suburbs, where he vents his rage by beating one of his five children **(Tom).**

Commentary

The line "He had done for himself in the office, pawned his watch, spent all his money; and he had not even got drunk" sums up Farrington's pervasive impotence. The beating of his young son in the story's final scene dramatizes his relationship to his children and, probably, his wife. Like "Eveline," this story shows how intractable Irish paralysis seemed to Joyce—impossible to ameliorate, much less escape altogether.

As ever, the author subtly holds the English and the Roman Catholic Church accountable. Farrington's coworkers at the law firm of Crosbie and Alleyne all have English or at least non-Irish names (Parker, Higgins, Shelley, Delacour), the woman who snubs him in the back room at O'Halloran's says "Pardon!" with a London accent, and just before arriving at home in Sandymount, Farrington passes the barracks where English soldiers live. More than in any *Dubliners* story yet, Ireland seems here to be a country under extended occupation by foreigners.

In the last scene of "Counterparts," Farrington's son reports that Mrs. Farrington is "out at the chapel." When Farrington begins to beat him, the boy desperately offers "I'll say a Hail Mary for you . . ." If not precisely to blame for Ireland's misery, the church certainly appears powerless against the forces paralyzing the culture.

Glossary

the tube   a machine for communicating within a building.

an order on the cashier   official permission for an advance on wages.

snug   a small private room or booth in a public house.

g.p.   a glass (half-pint) of porter.

caraway   a white-flowered biennial herb of the umbel familiy, with spicey, strong-smelling seeds. The seeds, when chewed, were thought to hide the smell of alcohol, and thus were offered to customers by turn-of-the-century Dublin bars.

manikin   a little man; dwarf.

instanter   without delay; immediately.

the dart   the solution.

stood . . . a half-one   bought a half measure of alcohol.

the eclogues   short pastoral poems, often in the form of a dialogue between two shepherds; the most famous are by the Latin poet Virgil.

my nabs   (slang) my friend or acquaintance.

Ballast Offices   the location of the Dublin Port and Docks Board, where the father of Gabriel Conroy (protagonist of "The Dead") is said to have worked.

Irish and Apollinaris   whiskey and soda.

too Irish   (slang) exceedingly generous.

chaffed   teased good naturedly.

tincture   a trace; a smattering.

small hot specials   whiskey mixed with water and sugar.

bitter   bitter, strongly hopped ale.

stood to   bought for.

smahan   a smattering; a smidgin.

barracks   buildings on Shelbourne Road for housing British soldiers.

Clay

Summary

It is Halloween night. After work in the kitchen of an industrial laundry mainly staffed by recovering alcoholics and ex-prostitutes, an older unmarried woman named **Maria** attends a party at the home of a man named **Joe.** Maria served as his nurse when Joe was a baby. While playing traditional Irish Halloween games, a blindfolded Maria chooses clay rather than water, a ring, or a prayerbook, signifying (at least according to Irish superstition) that she will die soon.

Commentary

Some critics have interpreted Maria as a symbol of Ireland itself (which would link her, unpredictably, with the pervert from "An Encounter"). Maria is poor and relatively forsaken. She is in thrall to the Roman Catholic Church (setting her alarm an hour earlier than usual so that she can attend All Saints' Day Mass the next morning), and she loses her gift while distracted by a "colonel-looking gentleman" who might represent England.

Maria is ignorant, as well. (Joyce believed that education in Roman Catholic schools had made the Irish ignorant, exacerbating the country's paralysis.) She does not seem to realize the significance of her choice in the Hallow Eve game. Joyce writes that "She felt a soft wet substance with her fingers and was surprised that nobody spoke or took off her bandage," rather than writing something like "She felt a soft wet substance, obviously clay rather than a book, ring, or water, and gasped at the thought of death foretold."

With regard to Joyce's system of color symbolism, the color brown (meaning decay) looms largest in this story. Maria's raincloak is brown, as is the hard hat of the man on the tram. And of course, the story's central image, the clay itself that superstition says may mean death for Maria, is probably brown, or brownish, as well.

Like "A Little Cloud" and "Counterparts," "Clay" employs the *limited third-person* point-of-view strategy. That is, although Maria does not herself tell the story, the reader is privy to her thoughts and no other characters'. (The story's narrator never tells anything that Maria *does not* know, as a traditional omniscient narrator almost certainly would.) The technique demands much of a reader (for example, figuring out that the "soft wet substance" Maria touches during the Hallow Eve game is the clay of the title), but the story rewards just this sort of participation. It also rewards repeated readings.

Glossary

barmbracks cakes, traditionally served in Ireland on Halloween, in which symbolic objects (a ring, for example) have been baked.

Ballsbridge a suburb southeast of Dublin.

the Pillar Nelson's Pillar; a memorial in north-central Dublin to Horatio Viscount Nelson (1758–1805), an English admiral. A comical anecdote told by Stephen Dedalus in *Ulysses* takes place atop the Pillar.

Whit-Monday the Monday immediately following Whit-Sunday, or Pentecost.

the Dublin By Lamplight laundry a Protestant-run business, the mission of which was to rescue prostitutes and drunken women; Maria merely works there, in the kitchen.

tracts on the walls religious texts posted for the edification of readers.

sure to get the ring likely to come upon the ring baked into the barmbrack, signifying that she will marry within a year.

a mass morning a Holy Day of Obligation, on which all observant Catholics must attend Mass.

has a drop taken has drunk alcohol.

Hallow Eve games referring here to a game in which players are led blindfolded to a table where saucers have been arranged: One holds a prayerbook, one a ring, one some water, and the fourth some clay. If the blindfolded participant chooses the prayerbook, he or she is supposed to join the priesthood or become a nun within the year. If the ring is chosen, marriage is foretold. Water means a long life, while clay means death.

"I Dreamt That I Dwelt"   a popular aria from the opera *The Bohemian Girl,* which is also mentioned in "Eveline." The song subtly connects this story with that one, perhaps implying that Eveline will likely end up like Maria.

her mistake   Maria has sung the song's first verse twice in a row.

Balfe   Michael William Balfe; composer of *The Bohemian Girl.*

A Painful Case

Summary

A solitary, effete bank cashier named **James Duffy** becomes acquainted with a woman named **Mrs. Sinico** at a Dublin concert. They meet regularly to discuss art and ideas, first at her house (with the full knowledge of her husband, **Captain Sinico**), and then at her cottage outside the city, where they grow close both intellectually and emotionally. When Mrs. Sinico reaches for Duffy's hand, however, he insists that they stop seeing one another. Four years later, Duffy reads in the newspaper about Mrs. Sinico's death, apparently by suicide. At first he feels revolted, ashamed that he ever considered her a peer. Then Duffy begins to feel guilty: Did his rejection of her result in Mrs. Sinico's suicide? Finally he identifies and empathizes with Mrs. Sinico, realizing that her aloneness mirrored his own—and that he is now more alone than ever.

Commentary

Theme

Like "Eveline," this is a story of missed opportunity, and true to its title, "A Painful Case" is perhaps even more agonizing to read than that earlier selection. Just as Eveline's fiancé presents her the chance to escape Ireland, Duffy is allowed a once-in-a-lifetime opportunity to connect with a kindred soul, Mrs. Sinico. Tragically (and typically), both are paralyzed: Eveline by guilt and fear, and Duffy by fear as well—fear that his fanatically orderly world will be thrown into disarray by shared passion. As in the earlier story, Joyce seemingly intends the reader to believe that such an opportunity will never come again.

Style & Language

In some ways, "A Painful Case" is the most sophisticated and complex *Dubliners* story yet, as it achieves its powerful effect through a deft combination of storytelling techniques and symbolism. As in "A Little Cloud," "Counterparts," and "Clay," Joyce employs the limited third-person point-of-view, allowing access to his protagonist's thoughts and feelings while keeping the reader distant enough from the main character to realize the errors of the protagonist's ways before the protagonist does. (The reader knows, for example, that it is a terrible mistake for Duffy to terminate his relationship with Mrs. Sinico.)

Unlike the stories "A Little Cloud," "Counterparts," and "Clay," however, "A Painful Case" includes information that was initially beyond the perspective of its protagonist. Because he does not speak with Mrs. Sinico for the four years immediately prior to her suicide, Duffy has no way of following what goes on in her life during that time, nor does the reader. Joyce includes the newspaper article documenting her death and the inquest that follows it, and the article retroactively shares Mrs. Sinico's life since of the past four years with Duffy and the reader. The author's use of this document to tell his story is an inventive way of surmounting his limited point-of-view strategy without violating its restrictive rules.

Joyce characterizes Duffy by means of his possessions: the picture-free walls of his uncarpeted room, and the fastidious, eminently practical manner in which he has arranged his books (by weight!). Though Joyce reveals that Duffy "abhorred anything which betokened physical or mental disorder," he doesn't really have to because he has taken care to *dramatize* Duffy's character. The reader can generalize about the man Duffy is based on the evidence presented.

Literary Device

The colors yellow and brown (which Joyce uses to indicate paralysis and decay) are everywhere in "A Painful Case"—in Duffy's uncarpeted floor, his hazel walking stick, and the beer and biscuits he eats for lunch. Even Duffy's face is brown: "the brown tint of the Dublin streets." An apple rots in his desk (that is, turns yellow and then brown), a symbol of Duffy's own decaying possibilities. The newspaper that announces Mrs. Sinico's suicide is buff in color, yellowish brown. The use of these colors by Joyce to symbolize decay and paralysis is consistent both within individual stories and across the collection as a whole. It thereby links the stories of *Dubliners* together, reiterating the common lot of the book's many disparate characters.

Glossary

Bile Beans a popular patent medicine in Ireland during Joyce's day.

the Rotunda a group of buildings on Rutland Square, one of which is a concert hall.

astrakhan a wool fabric with a pile cut and curled to look like a loosely curled fur made from the pelt of very young lambs originally bred near Astrakhan, a city and port in southwest Russia.

Earlsfort Terrace   the location of the Dublin International Exhibition Building, a concert venue at the time this story takes place.

Leghorn   a seaport in Tuscany, western Italy, on the Ligurian Sea (The Italian name is Livorno.)

Parkgate   the main entrance to Phoenix Park, the large public park in northwest Dublin.

the buff Mail   the Dublin Evening Mail, which was printed on buff (brownish-yellow) paper.

reefer   an overcoat; a short, thick, double-breasted coat in the style of a seaman's jacket.

the prayers   Secret prayers in the Roman Catholic mass between the Offertory and the Preface, read silently or quietly by the priest.

Sidney Parade   a train station on Sidney Parade Avenue, in the village of Merion, southeast of Dublin.

Leoville   apparently the name of the house in which the Sinicos lived.

a league   a temperance association; its members would have pledged to avoid alcohol.

the Herald   the Dublin Evening Herald.

Ivy Day in the Committee Room

Summary

On a rainy Dublin election day, **Mr. O'Connor** sits by the fire in the Committee Room after canvassing on behalf of a candidate for city council named Richard Tierney. O'Connor is visited by fellow canvassers and others, including the caretaker **Old Jack, Joe Hynes, John Henchy,** a suspended priest named **Father Keon, a delivery boy, Crofton,** and **Lyons** (possibly the Bantam Lyons mentioned in "The Boarding House" and in Joyce's *Ulysses*). Because it is also Ivy Day, the anniversary of the Irish patriot Charles Stuart Parnell, talk turns inevitably to Parnell; eventually, Joe Hynes delivers a poem he has written in the patriot's honor.

Commentary

Though it was Joyce's favorite of the tales in *Dubliners,* "Ivy Day in the Committee Room" is a difficult story for most American readers to comprehend, thanks to its excess of Irish slang and references to turn-of-the-century Irish politics. However, the fact that most of the story is told by means of dialogue rather than narrative—an unusual, even radical, approach at the time "Ivy Day" was written—should be appreciated. Like the prior story ("A Painful Case"), it also includes a document quoted at length in place of a conventional, dramatic climax. In "A Painful Case," the document was the newspaper article about Mrs. Sinico's suicide, while here it is Joe Hynes's poem, which he recites from memory.

Theme

The story is for the most part a naturalistic one with little in the way of overt symbolism, and yet "Ivy Day in the Committee Room" reiterates the themes of corruption and death introduced in the collection's first story, "The Sisters." The canvassers are working for money, rather than out of any particular enthusiasm on behalf of the candidate they support, and some of them seem actually to be contemptuous of Tierney. At the same time, they criticize others for having been paid off by the Protestant authorities: "Some of those hillsiders and fenians are a bit too clever if you ask me. . . . Do you know what my private and candid opinion is about some of those little jokers? I believe half of them are in the pay of the Castle." Some also suspect Joe Hynes of spying for the rival candidate in this election. Gossip is one of the motifs of "Ivy Day in the Committee Room." As soon as any of the characters depart the room, at least one of the others begins bad-mouthing him.

Ivy Day is the anniversary of the death of Charles Parnell, the Nationalist and "uncrowned king of Ireland" whom the Irish turned on when his affair with a married woman came to light—thus further delaying Irish independence.

Glossary

P.L.G. Poor Law Guardian; a welfare official.

cocks him up (slang) encourages an inflated self-image.

a sup taken had a drink of alcohol.

bowsy (slang) rogue.

tinker (Chiefly Irish and Scottish) gypsy.

shoneens (Irish) Irish who imitate English customs and behavior.

hunker-sliding (slang) shirking.

German monarch Edward VII (1841–1910); the king of Great Britain and Ireland (1901–10), son of Queen Victoria and Prince Albert, both of whom were of German descent.

Nationalist the Irish Parliamentary Party, which stood for Irish independence.

spondulics (slang) money.

musha (Irish-English) indeed.

úsha (Irish-English) the contraction of musha.

shoeboy a boot licker or insincere flatterer.

moya! (Irish) as it were!

had a tricky little black bottle up in a corner (slang) sold liquor illegally.

a decent skin (Irish slang) a good person underneath it all.

fenian   a member of a secret revolutionary movement formed in New York and Ireland to free Ireland from English rule. The movement was mostly active in the 1860s and continued until World War I.

Castle hacks   informers. The British ruled Ireland from Dublin *Castle,* in central Dublin just south of the River Liffey.

Major Sirr   Henry Charles Sirr (1764–1841); an Irish-born officer in the British army who put down rebellions in 1798 and 1803.

knock it out   get along financially.

goster   (Irish-English) gossip.

yerra   (Irish) really.

hop-o'-my-thumb   a short person.

the Mansion House   the official residence of Dublin's Lord Mayor.

vermin   malapropism for ermine.

Wisha!   (Irish-English) variant of musha.

a loan of   influence on.

Did the cow calve?   (slang) Is there a reason to celebrate?

Conservatives   the party in favor of maintaining union with England.

big rate-payer   a property owner.

Here's this chap comes to the throne after his old mother keeping him out of it till the man was grey   Because Queen Victoria ruled England and Ireland for over six decades, her son Edward VII did not inherit the throne until he was sixty years old.

The old one never went to see these wild Irish   Queen Victoria never visited Ireland (not, in fact, the case).

the Chief   a nickname for Parnell.

A Mother

Summary

An inexperienced Dublin impresario named **Mr. Holohan** arranges with **Mrs. Kearney** for her daughter **Kathleen** to accompany on the piano the singers at a series of four concerts. When the first three concerts are sparsely attended, Mrs. Kearney demands payment for all the performances before the fourth show, delaying the start of that evening's entertainment. Finally, Mrs. Kearney refuses to let Kathleen play during the second half of the concert because she has not been paid the entire promised fee.

Commentary

Theme

"A Mother" is a relatively straightforward and easy-to-read *Dubliners* selection that provides comic relief before the last two stories in the collection. The concert is literally paralyzed by Mrs. Kearney's greed until the Committee of the Eire Abu Society finds a replacement for Kathleen. In other words, although this story is light in tone, it nevertheless reiterates Joyce's main theme of paralysis.

Theme

"A Mother" also returns to the theme of corruption. The concerts staged by Holohan (who will reappear as Hoppy Holohan in *Ulysses*) are patriotic in nature, a celebration of Irish culture. And yet, Mrs. Kearney's only concern is the money promised to her daughter.

Although the goal of the Society is a renaissance of Irish culture and language, the concert series seems stillborn: "The poor lady sang Killarney in a bodiless gasping voice, with all the old-fashioned mannerisms of intonation and pronunciation which she believed lent elegance to her singing. She looked as if she had been resurrected from an old stage-wardrobe." Death, introduced in "The Sisters" and reiterated periodically ever since, reappears in "A Mother."

Literary
Device

Lastly, Joyce's color symbolism (with yellow and brown representing decay and paralysis) returns as well, linking this story with the others preceding it in a fashion that seems genuinely cinematic. Mr. Kearny has a "great brown beard," for example, and that brownness yields a consistency of appearance with the stories that have come before, as if the same cameraman shot all of them.

Glossary

Eire Abu   (Irish) Ireland to Victory.

went to the altar every first Friday   took communion on the first Friday of every month.

Skerries . . . Howth . . . Greystones   seaside resorts near London. "Eveline" included a reference to Howth.

Irish Revival   a movement, begun in the 1880s, that supported Irish culture in general, as well as a revival of Irish Gaelic as the country's national tongue. The Irish Revival will be the subject of a confrontation between Gabriel Conroy and a colleague in "The Dead."

to take advantage of her daughter's name   Ireland is sometimes personified as a woman named Kathleen ni Houlihan.

pro-cathedral   a temporary substitute for a cathedral.

charmeuse   a smooth fabric of silk; like satin in appearance but softer and having less body.

Brown Thomas's   a Dublin fabric shop.

the house was filled with paper   the theater was occupied for the most part by patrons admitted at no charge.

puff   an advertisement, review, or the like, as of a book, containing undue or exaggerated praise.

the dear knows   lord knows.

Maritana   an Irish light opera.

Feis Ceoil   a yearly festival of traditional Irish music.

the Freeman man   a reporter for the daily newspaper *The Freeman's Journal.*

Mrs. Pat Campbell Mrs. Patrick Campbell (1865–1940); a famous actress of the day.

"Killarney" a popular song by Michael William Balfe, composer of the opera *The Bohemian Girl* mentioned in "Eveline" and alluded to in "Clay."

fol-the-diddle-I-do a nonsense phrase.

Grace

Summary

After a Dublin tea taster and salesmen named **Tom Kernan** loses consciousness while drunk, his friends **Martin Cunningham, Jack Power, C.P. M'Coy,** and **Mr. Fogarty** gather in his bedroom to gossip about the church and persuade him to attend a retreat that they hope will renew his faith. In the story's last scene, the men attend the retreat together.

Commentary

This story is much like "Ivy Day in the Committee Room" in that it takes place for the most part in one room and is conveyed mainly by means of dialogue. Unfortunately, the dialogue, like that in the earlier story, is obscure to most American readers (though no doubt highly authentic). When the talk turns to ecclesiastical matters, mostly misinformation is shared by the participants; though their faith in God may be firm, their understanding of Roman Catholic dogma is shaky at best.

Here, Joyce repeats the theme of death—Kernan came near to killing himself when he fell down the stairs—and of corruption. Somehow, the purity of Christian faith in God has been corrupted by the institution of the Catholic Church, the author seems to say, and then further corrupted by types like Kernan's friends, who seem to mean well but misunderstand almost everything about their own faith. The way in which the priest at the retreat "dumbs down" the Bible for his audience is the final insult.

This is the most novelistic story in the collection, except for "The Dead." Not only is "Grace" longer than the stories that come before it, it also uses techniques such as three separate scenes and a truly omniscient point-of-view. Not only are the thoughts in Kernan's mind available to the reader, but his wife's and those of some of his friends are as well. These are techniques associated more with novels than with short stories. Fittingly, Kernan himself, as well as Cunningham and M'Coy appear in Joyce's great novel *Ulysses.*

Glossary

Grace   the unmerited love and favor of God toward mankind.

sha   (Irish) yes.

ulster   a long, loose, heavy overcoat, especially one with a belt, originally made of Irish frieze.

outsider   a horse-drawn carriage with two wheels.

Ballast Office   the location of the Dublin Port and Docks Board; in "The Dead," Gabriel Conroy's father is said to have worked there.

gaiter   a cloth or leather covering for the instep and ankle, and, sometimes, the calf of the leg; a spat or legging.

Blackwhite   apparently a renowned Irish salesman.

E.C.   east central.

the holy alls of it   (slang) the long and the short of it.

Fogarty's   a Dublin grocer.

her silver wedding   the twenty-fifth anniversary of marriage.

pale   a territory or district enclosed within bounds.

She believed steadily in the Sacred Heart   Mrs. Kernan displays an image of the sacred heart of Jesus in her home and takes communion on the first Friday of each month.

bona-fide travelers   inns and pubs were allowed to serve alcohol to travelers before or after hours during which it was generally legal to do so; thus, Mr. Harford and his friends "travel" to the suburbs so as to be allowed to drink legally on Sundays.

usurious   practicing usury; the act or practice of lending money at a rate of interest that is excessive or unlawfully high. Usury was forbidden for centuries by the Roman Catholic Church.

seven days without the option of a fine   a week in jail.

peloothered   (Irish slang) drunk.

True bill   a bill of indictment endorsed by a grand jury as supported by evidence sufficient to warrant a trial.

a crusade in search of valises and portmanteaus to enable Mrs. M'Coy to fulfil imaginary engagements in the country apparently M'Coy borrows luggage under false pretenses so as to pawn or sell it.

bostoons (Irish) rogues.

omadhauns (Irish) fools.

up here to Dublin from the countryside.

wash the pot (slang) to confess one's sins.

secular priests Roman Catholic clergymen with parish duties; as opposed to those priests who live apart from society in a monastery or house.

Father Tom Burke an internationally popular Irish preacher of the nineteenth century.

Orangeman strictly speaking, a member of a secret Protestant society organized in Northern Ireland (1795); here, the term is used simply to denote a Protestant and/or Unionist.

they don't believe in the Pope and in the mother of God a simplification of the ways in which the beliefs of Protestants differ from those of Roman Catholics.

Lux upon Lux obviously a misquotation, as even if the Pope had a motto, it wouldn't include English words.

Crux upon Crux obviously a misquotation, as even if the Pope had a motto, it wouldn't include English words.

a sod of turf under his oxter that is, each student was expected to help heat the school by bringing fuel. In Ireland, turf was burned to provide heat; "oxter" is slang for armpit.

up to the knocker up to snuff; passable.

ex cathedra (Latin) with the authority that comes from one's rank or office; often specifically with respect to papal pronouncements on matters of faith or morals that have authoritative finality.

Credo! (Latin) I believe!

Sir John Gray's statue a statue of a Protestant patriot located in north-central Dublin.

Edmund Dwyer Gray   the son of Sir John Gray.

lay-brother   in this case, an usher in a church.

speck of red light   the sanctuary lamp within a Catholic church.

quincunx   an arrangement of five objects in a square, with one at each corner and one in the middle.

surplice   a loose, white, wide-sleeved outer ecclesiastical vestment for some services, ranging from hip length to knee length.

Mammon   riches regarded as an object of worship and greedy pursuit; wealth or material gain as an evil, more or less deified (from Matthew 6:24).

The Dead

Summary

A professor and part-time book reviewer named **Gabriel Conroy** attends a Christmastime party thrown by his aunts (**Kate and Julia Morkan,** grand dames in the world of Dublin music) at which he dances with a fellow teacher and delivers a brief speech. As the party is breaking up, Gabriel witnesses his wife, **Gretta,** listening to a song sung by the renowned tenor **Bartell D'Arcy,** and the intensity of her focus on the music causes him to feel both sentimental and lustful. In a hotel room later, Gabriel is devastated to discover that he has misunderstood Gretta's feelings; she has been moved by the memory of a young lover named **Michael Furey** who preceded Gabriel, and who died for the love of Gretta. Gabriel realizes that she has never felt similarly passionate about their marriage. He feels alone and profoundly mortal, but spiritually connected for the first time with others.

List of Characters

Lily   Kate and Julia Morkan's housemaid.

Kate and Julia Morkan   Grand dames in the world of Dublin music, who throw an annual party at Christmastime.

Pat Morkan   Brother of Kate and Julia (dead).

Mary Jane Morkan   Church organist and daughter of Pat, thus niece of Kate and Julia.

Mr. Fulham   Kate and Julia Morkan's landlord.

Gabriel Conroy   A professor and part-time book reviewer; Kate and Julia Morkan's nephew.

Gretta Conroy   Gabriel's wife.

Freddy Malins   A drunken guest at the Morkans' party.

Ellen Morkan Conroy   Mother of Gabriel (dead).

T.J. Conroy   Member of the Dublin Port and Docks Board; father of Gabriel (dead).

Mrs. Malins, Miss Daly, Miss Power, Mr. Browne, Miss Furlong, Mr. Bergin, Mr. Kerrigan, and Miss O'Callaghan   Guests at the Morkans' party.

Bartell D'Arcy   A renowned tenor vocalist and a guest at the Morkans' party.

Constantine Conroy   A priest; brother of Gabriel.

Molly Ivors   A guest at the Morkans' party and a colleague of Gabriel's; she is involved in the movement to restore Irish language and culture to the island.

Patrick Morkan   Owner of a glue or starch mill, and father of Kate and Julia (dead).

Tom and Eva Conroy   Children of Gabriel and Gretta.

Michael Furey   Gretta's first lover, who died for the love of her.

Commentary

By general consensus, this is the greatest of all the stories in *Dubliners*—the longest, richest, and most emotionally affecting—and the story more than any other that points toward Joyce's career as one of the English language's greatest novelists ever. (He would follow this book with *A Portrait of the Artist As a Young Man, Ulysses,* and *Finnegans Wake.*)

Theme

The story reiterates the great themes of *Dubliners.* Gabriel's marriage is clearly suffering from paralysis, the condition of nearly all the characters in the collection. This accounts for his excitement at story's end when he believes that Gretta's passion relates to him and them, as

Character Map for "The Dead"

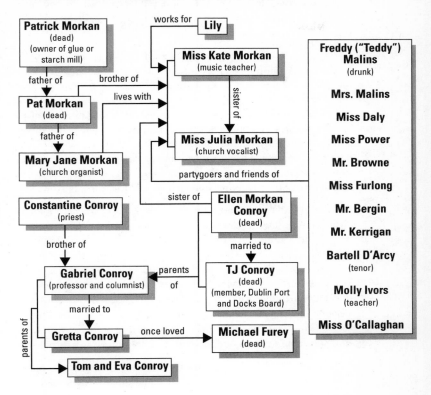

their marriage has decayed badly over the years. In this story, paralysis is represented as usual by the colors yellow and brown, but Joyce also employs the symbolism of snow and ice; after all, if something is frozen, it is motionless—paralyzed.

Thus, when Gabriel enters his aunts' party, "A light fringe of snow lay like a cape on the shoulders of his overcoat and like toecaps on the toes of his galoshes; and, as the buttons of his overcoat slipped with a squeaking noise through the snow-stiffened frieze, a cold fragrant air from out-of-doors escaped from crevices and folds." The symbolism returns at story's end, in the justly famous final paragraphs describing a snow-covered Ireland. Not only Gabriel but his entire homeland has been paralyzed, Joyce is saying (or, more precisely, revealing). Alternatively, at the conclusion of *Dubliners,* something connects Gabriel to his fellow Irishmen, a connection he had until that time disavowed.

Gabriel's paralysis is partly a result of his denial of and lack of interest in those fellow Irishmen, dramatized in his encounter with Miss Ivors. Like Kathleen Kearny in "A Mother," she is involved in the movement to restore Irish language and culture to the island. Gabriel writes a column for a newspaper opposed to Irish nationalism; indeed, he goes so far as to tell Miss Ivors, "Irish is not my language." Additionally, he tells her that he is uninterested in a vacation to the west of Ireland, preferring to holiday in Europe. She parries by calling him a West Briton—that is, an Irishman who identifies primarily with England, a cultural traitor—and this appears to be at least partly true.

After all, Gabriel plans to quote in his after-dinner speech from the work of the poet Robert Browning (an Englishman); when he finally delivers that speech, it includes extemporaneous remarks criticizing the "new generation" of Miss Ivors and her associates. Gabriel wears galoshes, fashionable in Europe, though more or less unheard of in Ireland. He earned his college degree at Anglican Trinity College in Dublin. When he thinks of going outside, what comes to mind is the snow-covered monument to Wellington, a British hero who played down his birth in Ireland. And speaking of monuments, another symbol of Ireland's inability to progress is Gabriel's grandfather riding his horse Johnny around and around the statue of William III, conqueror of Ireland on behalf of England. (The circle as symbol of pointless repetition was introduced in the stories "After the Race" and "Two Gallants.") Thus, as in many *Dubliners* stories before it, "The Dead" connects paralysis with the English. To summarize, Gabriel suffers from paralysis, at least partly because of his admiration for and attraction to things English.

Literary Device

Of course, Joyce also holds the Catholic Church accountable for Ireland's failure to move forward into modernity. Thus, in one of the story's most striking images (that of Trappist monks sleeping in their coffins, which is a myth, but that does not make it any less effective a symbol), Joyce portrays the most pious of clergymen as no less than the living dead, zombies among us.

Though "The Dead" includes much believable dialogue, it is the story in all of *Dubliners* with the most—and the most evocative— descriptions. For example, Joyce uses closely observed details to add to the reader's understanding of the story's characters, as in this descrip- tion of Freddy Malins: "His face was fleshy and pallid, touched with color only at the thick hanging lobes of his ears and at the wide wings of his nose." Not once but twice Freddy is described as "rubbing the knuckles of his left fist backwards and forwards into his left eye." As a result he is easily visualized, and despite Freddy's movement in and out of the Morkan sisters' party, the reader never quite loses track of him.

Joyce also uses description for pacing; the author cinematically cuts away to the ordinary objects within the room during the story's enormously dramatic penultimate scene. The result is that the already considerable dramatic tension of "The Dead" actually increases: "A pet- ticoat string dangled to the floor. One boot stood upright, its limp upper fallen down: the fellow of it lay upon its side."

As effective as the combination of theme, symbolism, dialogue, and description were in the prior story, "Grace," they mix here to yield some- thing even more impressive: a story that begins simply, builds slowly, eventually grows hypnotic in its power, and ends in a truly heartrend- ing burst of emotion. "One by one they were all becoming shades," Gabriel thinks of the people he knows and, until now, has taken for granted. "Better pass boldly into that other world, in the full glory of some passion, than fade and wither dismally with age."

"The Dead" is unforgettable, and it launches the reader from this collection of carefully wrought and closely joined stories (the world of *Dubliners*) into the world of Joyce's remarkable novels.

Glossary

had the organ in Haddington Road   played the organ at St. Mary's Church on Haddington Road, in south-central Dublin.

Adam and Eve's   a nickname for the Church of the Immaculate Conception, in southwest-central Dublin.

back answers   back-talk; insolence.

screwed   (slang) drunk.

palaver   flattery; cajolery.

Guttapercha   a rubberlike gum produced from the latex of various southeast Asian trees.

Christy Minstrels   a popular nineteenth-century American theatrical troupe featuring white performers made up to look like stereotypical black characters.

the famous Mrs. Cassidy, who is reported to have said "Now, Mary Grimes, if I don't take it, make me take it, for I feel I want it."   apparently the punch line to a popular joke of the day.

Quadrille   a square dance of French origin, consisting of several figures, performed by four couples.

the two murdered princes in the Tower   the two sons of England's King Edward IV, put to death in the Tower of London by their uncle, most likely, who would become Richard III.

tabinet   a poplin-like fabric made of silk and wool.

man-o'-war suit   presumably a child's costume intended to resemble a soldier's outfit.

curate   a clergyman who assists a vicar or rector.

Lancers   a nineteenth-century quadrille.

an Irish device   a Celtic emblem.

a crow to pluck   (slang) a bone to pick.

West Briton   a sympathizer with the English in Ireland.

the University question   the issue of Irish higher education. At the time the story is set, the country's main university, Trinity College, was Protestant affiliated, while the vast majority of the population was Roman Catholic.

go visiting perform a particular square dance figure.

embrasure an opening (for a door, window, and so on), especially one with the sides slanted so that it is wider on the inside than on the outside.

the park Phoenix Park, prominently featured in "A Painful Case."

Three Graces the three sister goddesses who have control over pleasure, charm, and beauty in human life and in nature.

Paris in Greek legend, a son of Priam, king of Troy. Of three goddesses (Aphrodite, Athena, and Hera), Paris chose to award the golden apple of Discord to Aphrodite; she, in turn, granted him Helen, wife of Menelaus, thus causing the Trojan War. A reference is made to golden apples in "A Little Cloud."

An irregular musketry a sound like many guns being fired, though not simultaneously.

"Arrayed for the Bridal" a song from *I Puritani,* an opera by Vincenzo Bellini.

refractory hard to manage; stubborn; obstinate.

the pope to turn out the women out of the choirs Pius X, pope at the time this story is set, excluded women from singing in church choirs.

the other persuasion Protestant.

To take a pick itself to have a bite to eat.

beannacht libh (Irish) goodbye.

blancmange a sweet, molded, jellylike dessert made with starch or gelatin, milk, flavoring, and other ingredients.

minerals mineral water.

the Gaiety a theater in south-central Dublin.

pantomime a drama played in action and gestures to the accompaniment of music or of words sung by a chorus.

a pass   free admission.

prima donna   the principal woman singer in an opera or concert.

slept in their coffins   Trappist monks were mistakenly believed to sleep in their coffins.

last end   mortality.

Fifteen Acres   a lawn or field in Dublin's Phoenix Park.

laid on here like the gas   made permanently available.

trap   a light, two-wheeled carriage with springs.

stock   a former type of large, wide, stiff cravat.

King Billy's statue   an equestrian statue of King William III, the Protestant conqueror of Ireland.

old Irish tonality   a pentatonic or five-tone scale.

the palace of the Four Courts   a building in north-central Dublin; the location of Ireland's central courts.

heliotrope   reddish-purple.

the statue   a statue of the Irish patriot Daniel O'Connell, known as "The Liberator."

toilet-table   dressing table.

cheval-glass   a full-length mirror mounted on swivels in a frame.

delicate   suffering from tuberculosis.

gasworks   a plant where gas for heating and lighting is prepared.

pennyboy   errand boy.

great with him   close to him, though not sexually intimate.

convent   a convent school.

Oughterard   a village north of Galway.

Nuns' Island   a district within the city of Galway.

Shannon   a river in west-central Ireland, flowing southwestward into the Atlantic.

CHARACTER ANALYSES

Unnamed Boy ("The Sisters," "An Encounter," "Araby")

The unnamed character who looks back on his boyhood while narrating "The Sisters" is a figure of central importance to *Dubliners* as a whole. He is the first character in the book who the reader gets to know from the inside. He serves as a sort of template for the main characters of the two stories that follow (and perhaps that of "The Dead," as well), and he makes concrete the collection's major themes by embodying opposite qualities.

The boy is a natural character with which to begin a book because he possesses so many qualities attractive to readers. First, he is sensitive—sensitive enough to experience a wide range of feelings in spite of his tender age, including apparently contradictory combinations like fear and longing (at the end of the story's first paragraph), anger and puzzlement (while falling asleep), and, especially, "a sensation of freedom" in response to his mentor's passing that surprises him and us. "I found it strange," the narrator says, "that neither I nor the day seemed in a mourning mood."

Second, he is intelligent—and not merely in the conventional sense of the word. Sure, he is brainy enough to absorb much of the arcane information shared with him by the priest. (It makes sense that he has grown into the articulate storyteller who shares the tale of Father Flynn's influence upon him.) But the protagonist of "The Sisters" also possesses an intuitive understanding of how other human beings feel, think, and act—*emotional* intelligence, you might call it.

"I knew I was under observation so I continued eating as if the news had not interested me," he says of the difficult moments after he has received the bad news about his teacher. Moments later, he fills his mouth with food so as to avoid an outburst directed at Old Cotter. He is probably right in his analysis of the situation. Clearly, it is the wrong time to stick up for himself, or for Father Flynn. At the house of mourning, the boy carefully observes his surroundings and acts appropriately, entering on tiptoe, pretending to pray when that seems the thing to do, refusing crackers for fear of making too much noise eating them, and, most of all, remaining quiet. Even adults can often be insensitive to the mood of their environment. The boy, however, always interprets the emotional tone of his surroundings correctly.

It is no surprise that a boy so sensitive, so intelligent, would find himself somewhat alienated from others—cut off, fundamentally, from his family and peers. He appears to lack altogether a connection with his uncle, much less Old Cotter, and it is said that he rarely plays "with young lads of his own age." Even when he is in the company of his aunt and the priest's sisters near story's end, the reader's main sense of the boy is that he is alone.

Finally, though the main character of "The Sisters" is no more in charge of his own fate than most children, he has an independent spirit and a desire to discover the true nature of things that cause him to search beyond the boundaries of convention. He quests, as far as he is capable of doing so, for that which he does not yet know. It is this characteristic that presumably brought him to the priest in the first place, and leads him to the house of the dead man and finally to Father Flynn's open casket. It is also this active, seeking quality in the boy that makes him most appealing to us.

In the unnamed boy at the center of "The Sisters," James Joyce found a prototype to which he would return in at least two other stories, if not three. Thus, the boys featured in "An Encounter" and "Araby" share fundamental characteristics of personality with the protagonist of "The Sisters," including the aforementioned sensitivity, intelligence, alienation, and questing nature. In Gabriel Conroy (the protagonist of "The Dead") Joyce introduces what seems to be a variation on this prototype: the unnamed boy grown up, married, and with children of his own.

Joyce also illustrates the major themes of *Dubliners* by contrast, showing their opposites in the unnamed heroes of the book's first three stories. Paralysis is countered by *movement,* as all three boys take little journeys—the first boy to the priest's house, the second to the Pigeon House, and the third to Araby. Joyce underlines the corruption of his adult characters by means of the *purity* of youth: When their stories commence, the three boys are untouched by death, sex, and the pain of love, respectively. Finally, though surrounded by the dead and dying, the three unnamed boys have by no means given up on life. On the contrary, as children, they are just beginning to experience the world and its wonders, and tend naively to welcome all that comes their way. In "The Sisters," "An Encounter," and "Araby," James Joyce offers the reader a first glimpse into the demoralizing world of Dublin and *Dubliners.* At the same time, he offers hope, in the form of his three unnamed protagonists. His own hope, perhaps, was that the reader would remember these boys during later, darker *Dubliners* encounters.

Gabriel Conroy ("The Dead")

Gabriel Conroy shares much in common with the unnamed boys at the center of the first three *Dubliners* stories. He is no less intelligent than his young predecessors, certainly, at least in the conventional sense of the word. He appears well educated, too; in fact, he earns his living from his intelligence and education, as a professor and book reviewer.

Partly as a result of these qualities, Gabriel is alienated, as well. Ironically, he is no less *alone* at the lively, crowded party thrown by his beloved aunts than is the protagonist of "Araby" on his solitary way to the church bazaar. While others appear gaily focussed on food and drink, music and conversation, Gabriel mainly obsesses over the speech he will make after dinner. Even while dancing with the "frank-mannered, talkative" Miss Ivors, he is preoccupied by things intellectual. It is also revealed during their conversation that he writes for a newspaper in favor of maintaining Union with Great Britain, and he spends his vacations abroad—both of which mark him as out of step with the passionately Irish guests at his aunts' party. Gabriel "coldly" refuses to travel to the west of the country, despite his wife's intense desire to do so. (Gretta comes from that part of Ireland.) "I'm sick of my own country, sick of it!" he finally admits to Miss Ivors, though he fails to explain why this is so. As a result, her feelings wounded, she leaves the party before dinner. Even while eating, Gabriel "set to his supper and took no part in the conversation."

He is disconnected from the people around him. "Gabriel hardly heard what she said" sums up his state. He looks out the window of the Morkans' drawing room and thinks "How pleasant it would be to walk out alone, first along the river and then through the park!" He is even cut off from the sensual pleasures offered by this celebratory holiday gathering. He foregoes sweets for dessert, eating a stick of celery instead—an insult, probably, to his Aunt Julia, who made the pudding. In short, he lacks the emotional intelligence of the protagonist of "The Sisters," and it is this very lack that will lead to his painful downfall at the climax of the story.

Educated and even refined, Gabriel nevertheless lacks true sensitivity. Though his blood relationship to the musical Morkan sisters and his marriage to the deeply passionate Gretta indicate that he might once have been finely attuned to the nuances of the world around him, Gabriel seems to have buried his emotions beneath a snow-like blanket of propriety. "She tried to make him ridiculous before people," he thinks resentfully of Miss Ivors, "heckling him and staring at him with her rabbit's eyes." He seems to have been a seeker once, a quester like the protagonists of "An Encounter" and "Araby." But Gabriel appears during the time at which "The Dead" takes place to have quieted the unsettled part of himself for the sake of comfort, safety, and status: "He . . . liked nothing better than to find himself at the head of a well-laden table." Later, Gabriel refers to "what vulgar people call stuffing." Appearances mean a great deal to him—more, perhaps, than what lies behind facades, the heart of things. His embarrassment (resentment, even) over the humble situation of his grandfather is striking.

Gabriel's lack of emotional intelligence, his insensitivity to the cues presented by the world around him, and his disinclination to search for the truth behind appearances eventually punish him. After first intellectualizing it ("He asked himself what is a woman standing on the stairs in the shadow, listening to distant music, a symbol of"), he badly misreads Gretta's impassioned response to Bartel D'Arcy's song. "Perhaps her thoughts had been running with his. Perhaps she felt the impetuous desire that was in him . . ." he theorizes. On the contrary, he has misinterpreted his wife's very essence, or ignored it altogether throughout their marriage. The realization devastates him.

The final evidence of Gabriel's link to the boy protagonists at the start of *Dubliners* is the self-knowledge—and the change—that this devastation appears to yield in him. For, remarkably, instead of bringing forth further paralysis, the realization of his emotional blindness ("He saw himself as a ludicrous figure . . .") encourages Gabriel to look outward—to begin to try connecting with all those from whom he has grown apart. He looks at Gretta "unresentfully," and cries "generous tears," tears reminiscent of those shed by the main character of "Araby" when he realizes his own folly. Then he begins to commune with the souls of the dead. Finally, in his mystical vision of a snow-covered Ireland, he begins the long and arduous process of connecting not only with those who have passed away, but with the living as well. Gabriel Conroy's quest has just begun.

CRITICAL ESSAYS

Themes of *Dubliners*

Even before its London publication in 1914, James Joyce's *Dubliners* caused considerable controversy due to the material in the stories that was obvious and accessible, available to even the most casual readers and reviewers. The collection all but overflows with unattractive human behavior: simony, truancy, pederasty, drunkenness (all of them in the first three stories alone!), child and spousal abuse, gambling, prostitution, petty thievery, blackmail, and suicide. The use throughout of the names of Dublin streets and parks—and especially shops, pubs, and railway companies—was seen as scandalous, too. (In the past, fiction writers had almost invariably changed the names of their short-story and novel settings, or discretely left them out altogether.) In fact, including these details delayed publication of the book by years, as potential publishers and printers feared lawsuits by those businesses mentioned by name. Disrespectful dialogue about the king of England, and even the use of the mild British oath "bloody," were thought by many to go beyond the bounds of good taste—and they did. In contrast to his status-conscious character Gabriel Conroy, James Joyce rejected good taste—one of the characteristics that mark his art as Modern.

A precedent existed for Joyce's warts-and-all approach, in the nineteenth-century French school of writing known as Naturalism, but no writer had ever been quite as explicit, or as relentlessly downbeat, as Joyce in *Dubliners*. To this day, despite a more liberal attitude in art and entertainment regarding the issues dramatized in the book (premarital sex, for instance, is hardly the taboo it was when "The Boarding House" appeared), many first-time readers are distracted by the unsavory surface details of nearly all the stories. This distraction can prevent them from appreciating *Dubliners'* deeper, more universal themes. It can be difficult to see the forest in this book for the blighted, stunted, gnarled trees. Of course, the forest is no fairyland, either. For Joyce's three major themes in Dubliners are *paralysis, corruption,* and *death.* All appear in the collection's very first story, "The Sisters"—and all continue to appear throughout the book, up to and including the magnificent final tale, "The Dead."

James Joyce himself wrote, "I call the series *Dubliners* to betray the soul of that . . . paralysis which many consider a city." Joyce believed passionately that Irish society and culture had been frozen in place for centuries by two forces: the Roman Catholic Church and England. The result, at the turn of the twentieth century, was one of the poorest, least-developed countries in all of Western Europe. And so images of paralysis recur throughout the collection obsessively, relentlessly, and without mercy. In the first line of "Sisters," and thus the first of *Dubliners* as a whole, it is revealed that Father Flynn has suffered a third and fatal stroke. Later, the unnamed protagonist of the story dreams of a gray face that "had died of paralysis," which is that of Father Flynn himself. This sets the tone for much of the material to follow.

The main character of "An Encounter" wants "real adventures," but is waylaid on his quest for the Pigeon House by a stranger who masturbates—a kind of paralysis because it is sex that does not result in procreation or even love. The *Pigeon* House itself is symbolic: A pigeon is a bird trained always to return home, no matter how far it flies. In "Araby," although the boy ultimately reaches the bazaar, he arrives too late to buy Mangan's sister a decent gift there. Why? Because his uncle, who holds the money that will make the excursion possible, has been out drinking. Drunkenness paralyzes too, of course. Eveline, in the story that bears her name, freezes at the gangplank leading to the ship that would take her away from her dead-end Dublin life. All three characters venture tentatively outward, only to be forced by fear or circumstance—by Ireland itself, Joyce would say—to return where they came from, literally or metaphorically empty handed. Indeed, characters in *Dubliners* are forever returning home, bereft: Think of the protagonists of "A Little Cloud," "Counterparts," and "Clay." The bereft Gabriel Conroy in "The Dead" never makes it home at all.

Yellow and brown are the colors symbolic of paralysis throughout the work of James Joyce. Note, for instance, that the old men in *Dubliners'* first two stories show yellow teeth when they smile. Joyce's other image of paralysis is the circle. The race cars in "After the Race" conjure images of circular or oval tracks on which starting and finish lines are one and the same, and indeed, the story's protagonist seems stuck in a pointless circuit of expensive schools and false friendships. In "Two Gallants" and "The Dead," characters travel around and around, never moving truly forward, never actually arriving anywhere. Lenehan in "Two Gallants" travels in a large and meaningless loop around Dublin, stopping only for a paltry meal and ending near to where he began. He is an observer, not an actor—and an observer of a petty crime, at that. In one of the most memorable images in the entire book, Gabriel's grandfather in "The Dead" is said to have owned a horse named Johnny who earned his keep at the family glue factory "walking round and round in order to drive the mill." One day, according to family legend, the "old gentleman" harnessed Johnny to a carriage and led him out into the city. Upon reaching a famous statue of King William, however, the horse could not be made to proceed onward, instead plodding dumbly in an endless circle around the statue. Gabriel acts this out, circling the front hall of the Morkans' house in his galoshes, to the delight of all. Conventionally, the circle is a symbol of life with positive connotations, as in wedding rings and Christmas wreaths. In *Dubliners,* however, it means an insuperable lack of progress, growth, and development. It means paralysis.

Joyce's second great theme here is corruption; that is, contamination, deterioration, perversity, or depravity. Because corruption prevents progress, it is closely related to the theme of paralysis—and indeed, corruption is almost as prevalent in *Dubliners* as paralysis. Again, Joyce introduces his theme at once. In the second paragraph of "The Sisters," the unnamed narrator mentions *simony* (the selling to its members by the Roman Catholic Church of blessings, pardons, or other favors), of which Father Flynn has apparently been guilty. The two stories that follow reiterate the theme. Certainly, perversity and depravity exist in "An Encounter," just as the narrator's unarguably pure love for Mangan's sister in "Araby" is contaminated—and effectively paralyzed—by his uncle's drunkenness. In fact, a subtheme of *Dubliners'* first three stories, as well as "A Little Cloud," "Counterparts," and "A Mother" is the corruption of childhood innocence—seen in the former stories from the child's point of view, and in the latter from the perspective of the corrupting adults.

Corruption returns in various guises throughout the book. In "The Boarding House," Mrs. Mooney hopes to earn money from the young woman living under her roof, and thus gives Polly "the run of the young men" there. In "Ivy Day in the Committee Room," the canvassers work for money, rather than out of enthusiasm on behalf of the candidate they support, and some of them in fact seem contemptuous of that candidate. "A Mother" returns to the theme of corruption, as the concerts staged by Holohan are patriotic in nature (a celebration of Irish culture), and yet Mrs. Kearney's only concern is the money promised to her daughter. Finally, in "Grace," the purity of Christian faith in God clearly has been corrupted by the institution of the Catholic Church—then further corrupted by types like Kernan's friends, who seem to mean well but misunderstand almost everything about their own faith. By discouraging him from drinking, Kernan's friends have probably saved his life, but they have done so by means of a sort of parody of real religion.

Joyce's third and last major theme in *Dubliners* is death. He links this theme closely to the prior two, and without much effort, as paralysis often precedes death, and corruption could be defined as resulting from a kind of spiritual or moral death. Once more, Joyce introduces his theme from the get-go: The events of "The Sisters" are caused by the death of Father Flynn, whose corpse the story's boy protagonist eventually sees face to face. Deaths are also implied in this story, and in "Araby"—those of the boys' parents, absent from both tales. Thereafter, death follows death in *Dubliners:* Dead is the priest who last lived in the house in "Araby"; Eveline's mother in "Eveline"; Mrs. Mooney's father in "The Boarding House"; Maria, perhaps, in "Clay" (the title of which symbolizes death itself); Mrs. Sinico (by suicide) in "A Painful Case"; Charles Parnell in "Ivy Day"; and finally Michael Furey and the other inhabitants of the churchyard in which he lays buried in "The Dead." Those are only the actual deaths in the book; add spiritual and moral deaths, and *Dubliners* grows as crowded with corpses as the Hades episode in Homer's *Odyssey.*

Paralysis, corruption, and death: In *Dubliners,* Joyce paints a grim picture of his hometown and its inhabitants. Keep in mind that he blamed the sorry state of affairs on outside forces—England and the church—rather than the Irish themselves. Looking back, the writer himself found the book insufficiently sympathetic to Dubliners' best qualities (hospitality, for example). He would address this deficiency in his masterpiece, *Ulysses,* which itself began as an aborted *Dubliners* story. Before that, however, he would tell the tale of a Dublin youth who vows to escape the paralysis, corruption, and death endemic to Dublin, a character based on Joyce himself whom he called Stephen Dedalus. Dedalus would be the main character of Joyce's thematically similar next book and his first novel: *A Portrait of the Artist As a Young Man.*

James Joyce and Popular Culture

Few books of the twentieth century are held in higher esteem by critics and academics than those of James Joyce. From the writer's early stories collected in *Dubliners,* to the almost impenetrable multilingual wordplay of his final book, *Finnegans Wake,* Joyce's writing is all but universally revered as the embodiment of the Modern in literature. These books, as well as *A Portrait of the Artist As a Young Man* and especially *Ulysses,* never fail to show up near or at the top of lists of great books written during the twentieth century. Without them, any version of the Modern literary canon would be incomplete. The writer himself has long since joined the pantheon of English-language storytellers, alongside Chaucer, Shakespeare, Milton, Austen, Eliot, Dickens, Hardy, and Conrad.

It is perhaps surprising, therefore, to discover the extent to which Joyce's passions by no means excluded the commonplace. The evidence lies in his books, though many readers miss it, distracted by his highbrow reputation. Logically enough, practitioners of popular art forms, like movies and rock-and-roll, have mimicked James Joyce's work.

Throughout his lifetime, Joyce maintained an abiding interest in what we today call popular culture. This might in part be explained by his humble beginnings. Though eventually Joyce held an undergraduate degree in modern languages (rather than some more arcane subject), he was born into an enormous lower-middle class family whose fortunes declined as he aged. Joyce's father John was a well-liked salt-of-the-earth type, a habitue of pubs and a talented singer of both light opera and parlor-songs (the pop tunes of the day). His influence rubbed off on Joyce, whose characters are forever buying drinks and bursting into song. Pubs are frequented in "Two Gallants," "A Little Cloud," "Counterparts," and "Grace." And melodies are sung in "Two Gallants," "Clay," "A Mother," and especially "The Dead." In fact, "Sunny Jim" Joyce grew into an inveterate bargoer himself, one known for his beautiful tenor voice and his tendency to dance home at closing time in the manner of Isadora Duncan. His favorite song was called "Oh, the Brown and Yellow Ale."

Joyce's characters read pulp fiction (the cowboys-and-Indians stories of "An Encounter") and true-crime books (*The Memoirs of Vidocq,* mentioned in "Araby"). They participate in auto racing and card playing ("After the Race"). They go shopping ("Araby"), dance ("A Little Cloud" and "The Dead"), and celebrate Halloween ("Clay"). Leopold Bloom, the hero of *Ulysses,* is famously obsessed by a newspaper advertisement (for Plumtree's Potted Meat), while his wife Molly (a professional singer) enjoys reading risque novels with titles like *Sweets of Sin.* In short, these folks do most of the things done by ordinary people of Joyce's day—and today. If he were writing during the twenty-first century, James Joyce's characters would undoubtedly be surfing the Net when not busy wandering the local mall.

Significantly, the inhabitants of *Dubliners* visit *real* pubs (Davey Byrne's, for instance) and stores (Fogarty's). They sing real songs ("I Dreamt That I Dwelt"), the music and lyrics to many of which can be located to this day. This melding of the imaginative and the actual was so unusual—so radical—that it resulted in the delay of *Dubliners'* publication for years, as publishers and printers worried about lawsuits by the owners of the establishments mentioned. In the meantime, Joyce had opened a movie theater during one of his rare return visits to Dublin; later, he would collaborate with the Russian filmmaker Eisenstein in an attempt to bring *Ulysses* to the screen.

It is no surprise that work so brimming with the pleasures of pop art and entertainment would inspire pop artists and entertainers in its wake. The crowd-pleasing novels of Stephen King and Danielle Steele, replete with Slurpees and Rolex watches, respectively, would be unimaginable without *Dubliners'* product placement. Films have been made of *Ulysses* and *A Portrait,* and not just a film but a Broadway musical adapted "The Dead." Movies structured according to associations made by their characters between memories and fantasies—words spoken and music heard—owe Joyce and his stream-of-consciousness technique a debt of gratitude, if not actual royalties. (An excellent example of this is Woody Allen's *Annie Hall.*)

In fact, royalties were very much at issue when the Irish art-rocker Kate Bush set Molly Bloom's famous soliloquy to music. Failing to receive permission from Joyce's estate, Bush wrote her own lyrics in the spirit of Molly and released the results in the song "The Sensual World" on her 1989 album of the same name. Another Irish performer, Van Morrison, mentions Joyce in not one but two of his songs. And many have theorized that John Lennon's free-associative lyrics in the Beatles' songs "I Am the Walrus" and "Come Together" were at least inspired by Joyce, though evidence of an explicit connection is so far lacking.

Mistaken for a highbrow by many who do not know his work and some who do, and considered by many acquaintances to have been a snob in real life, James Joyce remained in his literature fiercely egalitarian. Anyone genuinely shocked by this fact need only revisit the bawdy bits and topical references to be found throughout Shakespeare, another low-born writer whose characters frequent pubs and regularly burst into song—some of them the popular tunes of the Elizabethan era before the Bard adapted them. If Shakespeare's own favorite song wasn't "Oh, the Brown and Yellow Ale," it might have been something close. The obsessive references to *Hamlet* throughout *Ulysses* show that Shakespeare influenced James Joyce's fiction, written three centuries later. Similarly, Joyce's own approach inspires artists and entertainers today.

CliffsNotes Review

Q&A

1. *Dubliners* takes place in _____ at about _____.

2. The book is a collection of linked _____.

3. Before the start of "The Sisters," Father Flynn died of _____.

4. The unnamed main character of "An Encounter" plays hooky from school in hopes of traveling to _____.

5. The protagonist of "Araby" falls in love with _____.

6. Eveline's fiancé lives in _____.

7. In "The Boarding House," Mr. Doran is tricked into _____.

8. Little Chandler in "A Little Cloud" dreams of becoming a _____.

9. In "A Painful Case," Mr. Duffy finds out about Mrs. Sinico's suicide in _____.

10. In "The Dead," Gretta Conroy cries at the memory of _____.

Answers: 1. Dublin, 1900. **2.** Short stories. **3.** A stroke. **4.** The Pigeon House. **5.** Mangan's sister. **6.** Argentina. **7.** Marrying Mrs. Mooney's daughter. **8.** Poet. **9.** The newspaper. **10.** The death of her first lover.

Identify the Quote

1. There was no hope for him this time: it was the third stroke.

2. I wanted real adventures to happen to myself. But real adventures, I reflected, do not happen to people who remain at home: they must be sought abroad.

3. Gazing up into the darkness I saw myself as a creature driven and derided by vanity; and my eyes burned with anguish and anger.

4. She set her white face to him, passive, like a helpless animal. Her eyes gave him no sign of love or farewell or recognition.

5. His soul swooned slowly as he heard the snow falling faintly through the universe and faintly falling, like the descent of their last end, upon all the living and the dead.

Answers: (1) The unnamed narrator of "The Sisters," introducing (in the first line of the book) the theme of paralysis while describing the death of his mentor, Father Flynn. (2) The unnamed narrator of "An Encounter," verbalizing the need to escape from Ireland to avoid paralysis, corruption, and death. (3) The unnamed narrator of "Araby," describing his realization that the quest for a gift for Mangan's sister has been in vain. (4) The final lines of "Eveline," in which the title character is prevented by paralysis from leaving Ireland with her fiancé. (5) The final sentence of "The Dead" and of *Dubliners,* in which Gabriel Conroy communes with the dead of Ireland, and begins the process of communicating with the living.

Essay Questions

1. How is "The Sisters" an ideal story with which to open *Dubliners?* How is it less than ideal?

2. Are the protagonists of "The Sisters," "An Encounter," and "Araby" the same character? What do they have in common? How are they different?

3. What is the function of children in the stories from *Dubliners?*

4. How important are parents in the stories from *Dubliners?*

5. Focusing on "Araby" and "The Dead," write about adolescent love in *Dubliners.*

Practice Projects

1. Write a short story, set in your hometown, in the style of one of the stories from *Dubliners.*

2. Using a map of Dublin (hint: find one with a detailed index), trace Lenehan's route around the city in "Two Gallants." Although some of the pubs and restaurants mentioned no longer exist, almost all the streets and other landmarks can still be located.

3. Imagine that you are writing a screenplay for a two-hour movie combining "The Sisters," "An Encounter," and "Araby." You are limited to about 120 script pages. Which of the stories' scenes, characters, and events would you include and exclude? How would you arrange the material for maximum dramatic effect?

CliffsNotes Resource Center

Books

James Joyce, by Richard Ellman. This massive study by an acclaimed scholar of Irish literature and acknowledged Joyce expert has been called not just the last word on Joyce's life and times but one of the finest literary biographies of the twentieth century. Oxford: Oxford University Press, 1982.

Dubliners, by James Joyce, with an Introduction and Notes by Terence Brown. The endnotes to this edition of Joyce's book, by a professor at Trinity College, Dublin, provide the best guide to the many arcane and obscure cultural and geographic references in the stories. New York: Penguin, 1993.

James Joyce, by Edna O'Brien. This biography by O'Brien (an acclaimed Irish novelist in her own right) is brief, unconventional (with passages that mimic their subject's writing style), perhaps overly focused on sex, and as riveting as a first-rate contemporary novel. A collection of impressions rather than a work of scholarship per se, it nevertheless manages to communicate the essence of Joyce's life: the daily struggle to create works of literature that would last long after the writer was gone. New York: Viking, 1999.

Internet

The Brazen Head, www.themodernword.com/joyce/ — A stunningly detailed Web site, created and maintained by a passionate fan, on all things Joyce, including news, reviews, criticism, the writer's influence on other creators, and literally dozens of photographs (of Joyce, his family, and Dublin locales mentioned in his stories and novels). A highlight: the site's guide to music and lyrics inspired by Joyce's writings, featuring songs by the Beatles, Kate Bush, R.E.M., and Sonic Youth.

James Joyce Centre, www.jamesjoyce.ie/home/index.asp — The official Web site of the James Joyce Centre in Dublin, Ireland, with an excellent biography of the writer and links to information about official Bloomsday celebrations around the world.

Work in Progress: A Website Devoted to the Writings of James Joyce, www.2street.com/joyce/ — Links to e-texts, articles, maps, an excellent timeline of Joyce's lifetime, and contact information for face-to-face discussion groups around the world.

Films and Other Recordings

The Dead, directed by John Huston. The famous director's last film is a faithful adaptation of Joyce's last published short story—up to and including the well-known final paragraph from "The Dead," read over a shot of snow falling on rural Ireland. Among many affecting performances, Anjelica Huston's Gretta Conroy stands out for its subtlety and power, and for her pitch-perfect Galway accent. 1987.

Dubliners, read by Frank McCourt, Stephen Rea, Colm Meaney, and others. HarperCollins, 2000.

James Joyce: A Concise Biography. A videotape on Joyce's life and times. Famous Authors Series, 1996.

Index